2007

05

THE SILENT SPIRE SPEAKS

REV. M. RAYMOND, o.c.s.o.

THE BRUCE PUBLISHING COMPANY

MILWAUKEE

NIHIL OBSTAT:

    Fr. M. Charles English, O.C.S.O.
    Fr. M. Shane Regan, O.C.S.O.
    Censores Ordinis

IMPRIMI POTEST:

    ✠ Most Rev. M. Ignace Gillet, O.C.S.O.
    Abbas Generalis Ordinis Cisterciensis
    Strictioris Observantiae

NIHIL OBSTAT:

    John F. Murphy, S.T.D.
    Censor Librorum

IMPRIMATUR:

    ✠ William E. Cousins
    Archiepiscopus Milwauchiensis
    July 27, 1966

Library of Congress Catalog Card Number: 66–28857

© 1966 The Bruce Publishing Company
MADE IN THE UNITED STATES OF AMERICA

TO

My Brother

Fr. *J. P. F.*, S.J.

as tribute

in

HIS YEAR OF GOLDEN JUBILEE

1 9 6 5

With Warm Love and Glowing

Admiration for

The Way He Has Served Our Captain

C H R I S T

Other WORKS by FATHER M. RAYMOND, O.C.S.O.

Books

The Man Who Got Even With God

Three Religious Rebels

The Family That Overtook Christ

Burnt Out Incense

Love Does Such Things

A New Way of the Cross

God, a Woman, and the Way

These Women Walked With God

The Less Travelled Road

You

The Trappists, the Reds, and You

This Is Your Tomorrow . . . and Today

Now!

Your Hour

This Is Love

God Goes to Murderers' Row

The Mysteries in Your Life

Booklets

Is Your Home Like This?

Life Is Someone!

The God-Man's Double

You Are Leading a Dangerous Life

Are You?

Say "FIAT" and Remake Your World

Life Is a Divine Romance

You Can Set the World on Fire!

What Are You Doing to Jesus Christ?

Have You Met God?

What's Wrong? (College Graduates)

Doubling for the Mother of God

Whispers From the Wings

Running Off With God

Do You Want Life and Love?

Help God Be a Success

A Trappist Does a Startling Thing for You

For Your Own Defense

A Message From Those Killed in Action

A Letter to Mothers Whose Sons Are in the Service

Facts About Reason, Revelation, and Religion

CONTENTS

THE SILENT SPIRE SPEAKS

LISTEN!

"'SOME write for money. Some, for fame. Some — though very few — for art. Some, just for fun. But those reasons are not mine. My ink is sweat. I do not find dipping in that pot funny. . . . I write to preach. I write for propaganda. I write with a message — and for no other reason."

Thus spoke Peter Howard just two days before he died in Lima, Peru, while on one of his world tours to spread his propaganda, give his message, preach his plan. That plan was a plan for peace; but it called for a revolution that would involve every man, woman, and child in the world. It had nothing to do with Politics, national or international; nothing to do with Policies, domestic or foreign; nothing to do with world economics or power — but simply with the minds and hearts of us humans. For Peter Howard was the head of the world plan for Moral Rearmament. He sped through continent after continent pleading with men and women of every race, creed, and color to rearm — morally. But it was in America, and most particularly in the youth of America, that he placed his highest hopes.

I introduce this man, who died just two days after putting the finishing touches to a play he had entitled "Happy Death Day," for more reasons than one. It has often been asked: "Why does a monk write?" And even more pointedly: "Why does a silent Trappist-Cistercian monk write?" Peter Howard has given the

1

answer. At least, he has given *my* answer. I am a priest — I have to preach. I am a monk — I have a message. I am a silent Trappist-Cistercian — therefore, I have to shout: *"Listen — The Silent Spire Speaks!* — and what it says to you is vital."

I use Peter Howard for another reason: He wrote clearly. He spoke directly. He taught convincingly. He was simple, in the purest sense of that word — and burningly sincere. I have a passion for all those attributes. I am unqualifiedly convinced that for years now there has been a veritable conspiracy against clarity with the result that, today, no matter where you look — in art, in literature, and worst of all, but most of all, in life — there is heaped up confusion.

That is why it is so refreshing to meet a man like Peter Howard who put forth a plan of life the simplest can understand and the profoundest will find perfect. He said: "I take 'Thy will be done on earth as it is in Heaven' seriously — not as a pious hope, but as a passionate commitment."

That final word describes the man — and points the way for anyone else who would be truly human. "Commitment" has been one of those "in" words with many moderns for some time. But how many of these same moderns ever made a commitment? How many of them who did were ever as passionate about them as was Peter Howard? You cannot be commited to what is indefinite. You cannot be passionate about obscurities. Yet indefiniteness and obscurity mark much that is modern in painting, poetry, music, and dress; more still in politics, morals, marriage, and mores.

Many, as they read that last line will ask themselves: "What can a cloistered monk know about us moderns, let alone about our modern music, mores, morals, and dress?" I suppose most of you wonder just how we monks ever come to know anything about what goes on in your modern world. You know we live silent lives. You know we are cloistered. Some of you may know just how thoroughly cloistered we are here at Gethsemani; for you may be aware that we are hidden behind a circle of hills the locals call knobs; that we are situated a good half-hundred miles from the nearest large city; that we are securely separated from the nearby towns and villages by our own widespread property; then finally and firmly shut in by high grey walls of cinder block. And when you realize that we never see a newspaper, listen to radio, or look at television, you see how legitimate the question.

But you must never forget that we *do* receive some mail; that, occasionally, we *do* have visitors; and that every now and then we *are* presented with the latest publications in the fields of Theology, Philosophy, History, and Biography. It is from these three sources this book was born. For a few hours with such publications, some quiet pondering of the queries that come in through the mail, or some serious reflection on a day spent with visitors bring a monk not only abreast of the times, but even into a head-on collision with them. That is what happened to me recently. Then you must never forget that we monks have in abundance what you in the modern world almost totally lack: we have *leisure*.

Even I laugh as I look at that word. For it does seem absurd to use it about a life in which every hour, every moment, almost every split-second has its own call of duty. Yet, it is the apt, the exact, the most appropriate word possible to use in describing our life. For the Trappist-Cistercian life is very truly a life of leisure. We monks are the freest of all men — and that is the root meaning of the word *leisure:* freedom from occupation. We monks are not only free from the occupations, but more especially free from the preoccupations which consume the lives of so many today. We are free from all those concerns that eat the very heart out of so many of you; concerns, for instance, about an income that will give social status in the present and promise some social security for the future. Talk about Old Age Pension Plans. . . . But that is not what I was talking about, is it? I was talking about that real leisure which is afforded us in abundance, especially for what we call *lectio divina* — which means reading Sacred Scripture prayerfully, then quietly pondering the passage we have read. That is one of the surest, safest, and speediest ways of coming into intimate contact with God. For He, you know, is the Principal Author of Scripture. Contact with Him who is Subsistent Truth,

Beauty, Goodness, and Being gives us the touchstone we need in these days of confusion.

It is often startling to find, while reading Scripture, just how *ancient* many of our so-called modern problems are. Solomon does not seem to have been far wrong in his observation that "nothing under the sun is new." But who in the Age of the Atom and the Jet will take Solomon seriously? Not many. Most moderns prefer sophistication to wisdom. That may well be one of the fundamental reasons so many of them are missing the boat. And I do not refer to any luxury liner or excursion steamer; I refer to the Ark — not Noah's, nor even the one Moses had built, but to the Ark of the Covenant: to the very Ark of Salvation.

And that brings me back to Peter Howard and his passion for simplicity. We need that passion — all of us. For an insatiable craving to complicate everything seems to fever modern blood and be gnawing away at our very vitals. Now while it is true that complexity need not lead to confusion, it is equally true that it too often does. It always will, unless we know how to *simplify*. That we can do by aiming at the jugular; by striking to the roots. That is what Howard did when he said: "The real issue today is not between progressives and conservatives, not between free enterprise and capitalism, not between East and West, black and white, or even between capitalism and communism. No. The real issue is between those who believe that God made man and can change him, and those who believe man made God and can abolish him."

Does that sound exaggerated? Will some of you sophisticates dismiss Howard with your ever-ready sneer of "oversimplification"? It has always been a puzzle to me how anything could ever be *over*simplified. That prefix has always struck me as rendering the word self-contradictory. Yet, how many vital solutions have been dismissed by this bit of sophistication and very real sophistry! Still, I will let the sophisticates sneer at the simple, sincere Howard, then ask them what they will do when faced by the renowned scholar, Rabbi Abraham Heschel, and find him saying the very same thing, albeit in very different words?

Heschel stated his conviction that the major problem of the day is "the systematic liquidation of man's sensitivity to the challenge of God." Not quite as simple, is he? But that he holds the identical conviction is evident from the explanation he offered. "We are so infatuated with our great technological achievements," he said, "that we have forgotten the mystery of being — of being alive. We have lost our sense of radical amazement at sheer being. We have forgotten the meaning of being human, and the deep responsibility in just being alive."

That gives you some idea on the "liquidation." Now for the "challenge of God." The Rabbi observed that "Shakespeare's Hamlet said: 'To be or not to be: that is the question.' But, really, that is no problem. We all want to be. The real problem is *how* to be, and how *not* to be. That is our challenge; and it is that which marks the difference between the human and the animal. The animal wants to be. But for the human there is always the problem of *how* to be and how *not* to be. The meaning of God is precisely the challenge of *how to be*."

We monks know exactly what the Rabbi means by that last remark. For we know that we have been made in God's very "image and likeness" and, consequently, can never be fully human unless we are partly Divine. We are conscious of the challenge to "become what we are" every moment that we live. But Heschel sees modern man as so "overwhelmed by the power he has achieved, that he now has the illusion of Sovereignty; has become blind to his own situation, and deaf to the question always being asked of him."

The Rabbi says exactly what the Rearmament man said: men are "abolishing God." That is what his "illusion of Sovereignty" means. He does not like it. Neither do I. Nor must you. These two men have brought this cloistered monk not only *abreast* of the times, but into *head-on* collision with them. For no man can remain silent when he clearly sees that this "illusion of Sovereignty," which can never diminish Divinity, can very definitely destroy humanity. To "abolish God" is an utter impossibility. But to destroy man. . . . Is it already being accomplished?

Heschel intimates it is. "Why do we not see the writing on the wall?" he asked, then accused modern man of a complacency that is selfish and cruel, and an apathy that is actually destroying mankind.

That is going for the jugular. For he points to the frightening fact that we are already doing, almost with complacency, things none of us want done. No one wants nuclear bombs; but we stockpile them. No one really wants satellites orbiting our globe; but we spend billions to put them in orbit. No one wants the war in Viet Nam; but we fight it. Apathy is behind all these activities. No wonder Heschel cried: "It is as if we had lost all vision, all wisdom, and there is very little comfort."

But he does not totally despair. He has hope in the very thing that drove Howard on with such passion. The Rabbi, too, calls for a world revolution — to achieve peace. "We ought to mobilize *all* our forces *everywhere*," he says, "to achieve world peace. The problems are complex," he admits; for "power is involved, industry is involved, trade is involved." But then he asks: "But what about life itself? What about humanity?"

But do not think it is my purpose to enroll you in the ranks for Moral Rearmament, or involve you in world revolution. I have introduced these two men to show you one source of a cloistered monk's information not only about what is going on in the world, but also what is not. Not enough clear thinking is going on. Not enough listening . . . the kind Howard called for when he cried: "Wake up! There is yet time — and there is a way to begin again. It is by accepting *absolute* standards of morality and by being *still* long enough each day to *listen* to the voice of God — then *doing what He says.*"

Do not pass that off as "Piety"! For no thinking man will question the fact that much of your world's confusion stems from lack of stillness enough to allow man to focus his eyes sharply enough to distinguish reality from realism, and lack of silence enough to allow man rightly to hear. Too much sound deafens. Too much light blinds — to the world's only True Light.

That is why I love our darkness. We have it aplenty. For,

usually, we are putting out our lights when most of you are just putting yours on. We retire at 7 p.m. in the winter, and at 8 during the summer. That is why we are putting on our comparatively dim lights when some among you are just putting out the most brilliant in your world. We rise at 2 a.m. on Sundays and feasts; at 2:15 all other days. The world is dark at that hour — both summer and winter. But, oh, the things that are seen in that darkness. For it is a darkness made luminous by the Light of Faith, but more so by Him who said He was "The Light of the World." It is He whom we meet every morning under our silent spire — and it is He whom we hear. For in that luminous darkness we not only lift our voices in the praise of God but listen attentively to the God we praise.

That marks our second advantage over you outside — our freedom from din. Yours is a noisy world — so noisy that, in it, actually, it is difficult to hear. Oh, I know you get used to it; so used that you are only dimly conscious of the traffic noises coming from both the ground and the air. I know you become only semiconscious of the ceaseless flow of jazz and chatter that comes from the never silent radio. I suppose many of you are utterly unconscious of the cries that come from your blaring headlines and the loud shouting from your various advertisements. But it is all noise. It all has its effects. Those decibels are diabolically well calculated to keep you from being even subconscious of the one sound Peter Howard wants you to hear — the sound we hear in our dark silence: not only the Voice of Christ, but the voice of conscience.

Howard and Heschel would have been enough to make me cry *"Listen!"* but they have not been alone. Just today, from three different parts of our country, I received mail that confirmed these two men and showed how some are trying to "abolish God." From Florida, California, and New York came letters telling me that *"God is dead."*

One of my friends down in St. Petersburg, Florida had heard it on TV. She sorrowfully reported how a choir somewhere up in the Carolinas was heard singing: "God is dead." From Long

Beach, California, came the story of how a theology professor in some school in Georgia had just made the headlines by announcing to his class: "God is dead." I chuckled as I read that absurdity; for it brought back a similar absurdity of my student days of the long, long ago. Sophisticated professors of psychology were then teaching that man had no soul. Psychology without a soul is absurd enough, but theology without God is the height of absurdity. I might have shrugged it off as I reminded myself of Solomon and his remark about the sun seldom shining on anything new, but then I opened a letter from New York. This correspondent sounded excited. He had previously expressed his admiration for young Deitrich Bonhoeffer, the Protestant theologian who had died at the hands of the Nazis because of his unquenchable anti-Fascism. But now my young friend was disturbed; for he had just run across some lines Bonhoeffer had penned while in Tegel Prison, Berlin, to the effect that "We are now heading toward a time of no religion at all. Men as they are, simply cannot be religious any more." My young friend asked: "What does he mean — that God is dead?" I laid the letter down saying "No, but man is close to it."

I had met Bonhoeffer before. I knew he was considered by some to be "the most provocative and most influential apostle of Christianity in the twentieth century." Yet I also knew how newspapers and magazines had snapped up his sensational-sounding phrases and told readers how this young apostle of Christianity had called for "non-religious Christianity" in our present-day world which, he claimed, was an "adult world," a "world come of age," in which there was no room for "religious Christianity."

Those are arresting phrases. They make excellent headlines. But in a world where so many read as they run what confusion they can generate! Bonhoeffer did not mean what such reports would make him mean. Actually, I believe the young theologian fell into a fallacy as old as man: that of judging the many from the few, or to put it a bit more technically, of having a conclusion far wider than his premises will permit. Bonhoeffer took those who were guilty of what the thinking man recognizes as "formalism" and "pharisaism" — and from them fashioned his description of present-day "religious Christianity." Anyone, sincere about religion, wants to banish formalism and pharisaism; but no one sincerely wants "non-religious Christianity." But see what slanted reporting can do. My contention about there being a conspiracy against clarity is not mere rhetoric. I dare go so far as to claim the conspiracy is now above ground and has become a veritable crusade for confusion. And nowhere is it being waged with greater efficacy than in the Press. Just try to imagine what a hold those vivid, vital, colorful, and catchy phrases of Bonhoeffer's about "adult world," "world come of age," "non-religious Christianity" will take on the unreflective in your modern, noisy world — and their number is legion. Yet, what Bonhoeffer was really calling for was sincerity in our worship of God and our following of Christ. In fact, I am using him to show you the method I am going to follow in this book and the enemy of yours I hope to vanquish. Bonhoeffer once said: "To be simple is to fix one's eye solely on the simple truth of God . . . especially at a time when all concepts are being confused, distorted, and turned upside down." That is the present time.

Look at the facts. Take the report on that Theology Professor who was teaching that "God is dead." Sounds like anything but Theology, doesn't it? Yet the man was but trying to exegete St. Paul. He was urging his students to be anything but irreligious. For the passage on which he bases his theory begins: "Be of the same mind as Christ Jesus . . ." (Phil 2:5). Yet the Press comes out with "God is dead." Slanted? Of course the reporters had some grounds for their report. The Professor went on to the line where Paul says Christ "emptied Himself." In Greek the word for empty is KENOSIS. This passage gave birth to the "Kenotic Theory" which is a heresy as old as the Press. It was born just about the time Gutenberg's children were playing with the blocks which gave him his idea for a printing press. I feel sure the Professor was stressing the humility of Christ. But the Press would have him "abolishing God." Crusade for confusion?

One more example. This time from a Catholic priest. Father Alfred Delp, S.J., died, it can be said, for God and for man. He was executed by the Nazis because of his connection with a group that was planning to establish a Christian social order for Germany once Hitlerism had passed. From his prison cell he gave us what *The Boston Pilot* has called "One of the great human and spiritual documents of our time." But in the secular press we read such extracts as "Man today is profoundly Godless. This is a basic fact affecting both his judgment and his decisions. But it goes even deeper than that; for modern man is no longer *capable* of knowing God."

Father Delp did write those lines. Taken by themselves they can only mean that, for modern man, God *is* dead. Yet, they are taken from an essay on *The Education of Man* in which Father explicitly states that it must be "a purposeful education towards perfect manhood, an education towards God." That is what I mean by a "crusade for confusion," why I burn with a passion for clarity. Clarity can mean not only your salvation as man — but, in a very true sense, the very salvation of God for men. That is why I cry: *"Listen!"* I have news for you — Good News. In fact the very best news possible: *The Silent Spire Speaks,* and what it says will make your life not only livable, but lovable; for it will fill it to the full with *meaning.*

But before plunging into the silence in which we can hear, let me introduce you to the third source of a cloistered monk's information about the world beyond his cloister. It is the most pertinent as far as this book is concerned; for it proves that "everything that rises must converge." I am not thinking only of Flannery O'Connor or of Teilhard de Chardin as I write that. I am looking into myself. Books that told of God being dead set something rising in me. Letters that told the same, set something more rising. But it was really two visitors who made all the rising converge into this book. They were college freshmen; one at Northwestern University, the other at the University of Notre Dame. They had the same tale to tell — all about God being dead; but they told it in different ways.

There is something else that Peter Howard once said which has pointed relevance here: "There will be no Great Society without great men and great women. But men are not made great by big guns, big incomes, big bellies, big appetites for sex and comfort. No. We need a big aim and big decisions — and discipline enough to fulfill them." Did he have hope that we would acquire that discipline? He was anything but a pessimist, yet speaking in Town Hall Forum in Los Angeles he said: "I thank God on my knees each day for the strength of America. But without a Faith all men can understand and love, without a discipline to match that Faith, America may yet become a dead knight in armor." Then later at Iowa State University: "With all the force at my command I say that the moral compromise now taking place on the campuses of America will lead directly to the death of freedom unless America wakes up."

The campuses of America hold the future of America because they hold America's youth. It was among young people that I spent many years before coming to the cloister. So I am not utterly ignorant of what makes them tick. Never expect any experienced priest to get highly excited about any reports on the excesses of youth. We know something about seed time and the "sowing of wild oats." So, while such "sowing" will never get us overexcited, we will always know, and show, some concern about the harvest. We well know that some youths will always be prone to "raise Cain." But since Cain had a brother, we are never without some concern for Abel. But now this not-so-young priest must confess that today's youth has him disturbed. It is not the "wild oats" or their "Cain" that bothers me; it is their boredom. Yes, I have found them *bored*. Not blasé, mind you. Back in the twenties and thirties youth posed as blasé. But these youngsters in the sixties are not posing. They are actually bored — bored with just about everything: life, school, religion, society, the nation, war, peace, and with every movement afoot. That is disturbing.

Now note I am not talking about teen-age crime, youthful drug addiction, the heavy drinking among adolescents, nor the high accident rate among youthful drivers. I am talking about what is behind and underneath all that. I am talking about what is deep within youth itself these days: unrest, and very real confusion.

I am acquainted with all the causes that have been assigned for this condition: the unsettled times, the shadow of the bomb, the ever accelerating automation, the very affluence of society itself. I have heard all about "parental delinquency," too. But I say that while all of these contribute, no one of them, nor all of them together give the underlying cause. I say the basic cause of all this boredom lies in *meaninglessness*.

Never undersell youth. It is more serious than many an adult believes, and deeper far than many an adult suspects. Youth is keen. It recognizes phoniness immediately, and wants nothing to do with it. And, as you well know, there is much phoniness, in our so-called adult world today. Hence, the unrest of youth, its dissatisfaction, its boredom. To them life looks *meaningless*.

Youth's biggest quest is not for thrill, kick, excitement. They are not always seeking what so many of them refer to as a "charge." No, their most serious search is for *meaning*. They want to know the meaning of their own personal existence; the meaning of life as a whole; the ultimate meaning of their present being, and of the being of so many that are now present to them. How can they find it in our culture and machine-directed civilization that so blatantly tells them that "God is dead"?

Just what is going on in the classrooms of America, I do not know. But of this I am certain: there is not too much *clarity*. Youth is not being taught the meaning of man, the meaning of life, the truth about being — with any *clarity*. And yet our civilization, which we used to call Christian, but which is now called Western, is based on *clarity* —on utmost clarity about man, his Maker, and the meaning of both. Our forefathers lived in no obscurity about ultimates and absolutes, about fundamentals and finals. If you want to read a scathing condemnation of the turbidity of modern thought, and the toxic state of present-day perceptiveness, read the opening paragraph of the Declaration of Independence. Our

Founding Fathers stated incontrovertible truth with utter clarity. We deem ourselves aeons beyond them in knowledge, and yet they found "self-evident" what I find youths from college campuses flatly claiming to be obscure and practically impossible to attain. Our Founding Fathers held as "self-evident" that "all men are created equal. . . ." How many modern sophisticates would ever reach the word "equal" in that phrase? How many of them could say "created"? Yet the Founding Fathers went on with what was to them "self-evident"; namely, that all men have been "endowed by their Creator with certain unalienable rights. . . ."

That clarity has vanished from our campuses if I am to judge from the visitors I have had — I take them to be typical rather than exceptional. Tom came to me from Northwestern. It was soon evident that he had heard little about the Creator, let alone that He was the Source of every "unalienable right." Yet Tom was loud, clamorous in fact, for some of those rights, at least his "right" to the exercise of his "liberty," and his "right" to "life." But Tom soon showed me he had no idea what "life" is, let alone what "liberty" is for. How could he, when he had no clear idea on what *man* is? You should have seen his face when I said: "The meaning of man lies outside of man." Would our Founding Fathers have gasped and gaped as this youngster did? Hardly. Not when they held as a "self-evident truth" that man has a *Maker;* that man was *created;* and that man's goal is *"happiness."*

Tom is just going out of his teens. But before he does he wants to write a novel on adolescence. This is the way he put it to me — in writing; for I found him too facile a talker. In conversation it was difficult to pin him down to a point. But in correspondence — "what is written is always there." He wrote: "I'm not anti-religious, anti-God, anti-anything; I'm just pro-humanity. I believe I'm doing much more for humanity than any hermit holed up here in Kentucky. My work? — I'm writing a novel about adolescence. I'm struggling furiously to get it finished while I'm still adolescent; for the people I know, the person I am, and the things I perceive are not the kind of people, persons, or things found in any account of 'The Teen-Age Problem' or books like that. I'm trying desperately to capture the sight-sound-odor-touch of the intelligent, sensitive, screwed up people who are unfortunately, under twenty-one and, therefore, are useless in the eyes of society."

That sounds like anything but boredom, doesn't it? Tom sounds electric with life, with interest in his own. He seems to have purpose. Unquestionably he has drive. But look at him more closely, and listen more keenly. He says he is going "to show the motivations of this group, their methods for drive-reduction, their behavior in all matters of social intercourse, bewilderment, isolation, hate, affection, fear, love. I'm going to give their views on war, sex, religion, love, marriage, Joyce, and birth control. In other words, the world as they see it."

He himself admitted that this was a rather large order, so he settled for "relating the story of two adolescents, weighed down and drowning in humanity and, cramped by their sensitivity, struggling desperately to pull one another to the surface, only to realize they are actually pushing each other down."

Some adults, I know, would refuse to take this youngster seriously. I think they are wrong. Tom is not exceptional; he is typical of an almost countless number of college boys. I see him — and them — as searching for meaning. Tom proved to me the need for even teen-agers — I should say *especially* teen-agers — to listen to the Silent Spire, and hear what it has to say. The truths it tells will keep them from being as truculent as Tom, save them from "drowning in humanity," and free them from the confusion of thinking they are "struggling for the surface" when actually drowning in the depths!

But it was a freshman from Notre Dame who finally made me sit down to this typewriter; for he showed me the vital necessity for *clarity* in the modern world concerning basic truths. He also showed me how an *apologia* for our Trappist way of life is actually an *apologia* for the existence of God — which would be blasphemy anywhere but in our blundering, bewildered modern world — as well as being an *apologia* for man and his meaning.

Alexie is no teen-ager. He is older, I would surmise, than any freshman at Notre Dame, and older even than many of its recent graduates. He is not an American. His home is in Southern Rhodesia; but he has travelled most of the world, and received his pre-college education in Europe and Africa. No chance for any "ghetto-intellect" in this young man. When he came to me afire with enthusiasm for Friedrich Wilhelm Nietzsche — the loudest of all those who have proclaimed that "God is dead" — yet so ignorant of the man who proved not only that God lives but is the God of all the living, that when I mentioned St. Thomas to him, Alexie thought I was referring to the "doubting Didymous" and not to that "Dumb Ox" whose mental brilliance has burned away so many doubts — Thomas of Aquin — I saw that something drastic had to be done. I set him listening to the Silent Spire. He finally got its message.

I have looked at, and listened to, this same Spire for all of thirty years now. I have seen it under every kind of sky, and heard it in every kind of weather. I have looked at it long under sunlight, moonlight, starlight and amidst gloom. I have seen it standing solitary against an empty blue heaven, standing solidly against a howling gale, standing stately under a falling snow and serenely amidst driving rain. And its silence has always spoken to me and told me those truths that make life meaningful, give calm, courage, and confidence when our whole world shakes as if Atlas had shrugged. Those are the gifts I would give you. Those are the truths I would have you know.

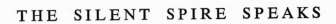

THE SILENT SPIRE SPEAKS

ONE · PLAYING...WITH FIRE!

A L E X I E walked in on me Easter Eve. I was not exactly surprised; but, then again, I was not exactly prepared. I knew he was in the country — had been for months. I was sure that, sooner or later, he would show up at Gethsemani. But because Easter Eve was so much later than I had expected, there was an element of soonness and surprise in his unannounced appearance. His parents had cabled me from Leopardstown, their estate just outside Salisbury in Southern Rhodesia, in early September, telling me that Alexie was to enroll as freshman at Notre Dame that same month. But a beautiful fall withered its way into winter, and winter had now melted into a delightful spring before I laid eyes on the young man. My first sight of him stirred very pleasant memories of both his parents; for he looked at me from out the same, wide-set, smiling Irish eyes that are his mother's most attractive feature, and he towered over me with the same height, build, and noble bearing that characterizes his Austrian father.

That word "noble" is apt; for had the Empire of Franz Joseph perdured I would have had cause to address Alexie as "Count." But, things being as they were, my first appellation for him was "Stinker!" I meant it as playful, of course; but because he had been so slow in getting to Gethsemani, there was some peeve in my playfulness. But, before the visit ended, that flippant term, which hardly conceals insult, became my favorite mode of fond address for this young man whose mental processes reminded me so much of my own. I saw so much of my former self in this youngster from Africa that I fell into my old habit of what I used to name my "Socratic method:" I answered many of his questions with two more of my own, and thus gave reply to his inquiry by forcing him to rethink his query and thus answer himself.

Two of a kind actually made a full house that Paschaltide; for no matter where Alexie and I were: in the Guest House, the Gate House, or the Retreat House, we always made it a house full of discussion. But if ever my favorite aphorism: "Discussion leads to Discovery" was proved, it was proved that Paschaltide.

For three days I fenced with this young man intellectually. He is Austrian-Irish — but, as far as I could judge, much more Irish than Austrian; for I found Irish impatience, impulsiveness, and impetuosity in many of his mental processes — not to mention flashes of Irish "impishness." He left me, after three days, mentally limp, but with a memory literally writhing with vivid impressions of youth and vital insights into its troubles; but a memory moving also with admiration for youth's honesty and its craving for the genuine. But more particularly, Alexie left me with an intellect alive with the realization that the truth our Silent Spire speaks is more timely than tomorrow's newscast — and must be told now.

It began innocently enough when he gave me his adult, and shall I say, European, reactions to the football frenzy he had found at Notre Dame the past fall. He, although an able athlete himself, characterized our American game as a "spectator's sport" — and the campus enthusiasm as "somewhat childish." I could have blushed; for, despite three decades of cloistered life, I believe I can still grow enthusiastic about a college game. Perhaps it was that which caused me to shift the topic of conversation and get into discussion about his courses at the University. He mentioned Philosophy, Theology, Sociology, and Physics with enough enthusiasm to set me questioning him on some of the disputed doctrines in each subject. I can see now that I was indulging myself.

I was nostalgic for the days when classes of college youth sat in front of me, and it was joy to prod their intellects into further and further probing. Alexie responded to all my prodding with a willingness that had me envying his present-day professors. I saw that I had an exceptional student in my presence. His six or seven years away from classrooms had so whetted his appetite for knowledge that he was now voracious. All went very well until I asked about his course in Literature. It was then we locked horns. He was exclamatory about Friedrich Wilhelm Nietzsche. It was not long before I also was exclamatory.

I smile now as I recall the heat with which I ended our discussion Easter Sunday night. I had been attracted at first by the boy's enthusiasm for the reading that had been assigned him. I grew amused to find him so much in admiration of this German pseudo-philosopher. But as he grew more and more enthusiastic with each new quote or comment I grew concerned. Finally I said: "Alexie, with shelves on shelves of truly sound literature up in that new multimillion-dollar library of yours, why you should be glutting your mind with this mad man . . ."

Perhaps Alexie did not take note of the light in my eyes, though I thought there was sufficient fire in my voice to warn anyone. At any rate, he broke in with a chuckle and the query: "Oh, Father — aren't you manifesting what they call the 'ghetto mentality of the Catholic'? Why call Nietzsche a madman?"

"Because he was!" I answered. "Further because I now want to alert you to fact — and one fact is that in using that phrase about 'ghetto mentality' you are manifesting less maturity than you have shown all day and all evening. You are parroting some of the *avant garde,* Alexie, and you do not need to parrot anybody. God has given you enough intelligence to keep you from ever entering among the so-called *intelligensia,* where, alas, you will not find too much real intelligence. That phrase 'ghetto mentality' is not as brilliant a coinage as many of the *avant gardists* think. And if they ever come to rethink it — something I fear those boys seldom do! — they will blush at its inaccuracy, superficiality, and slander. When I attack you for reading Nietzsche while still a freshman, and for being so enthusiastic about the man, I am but manifesting a Catholic mind and its assessment of objective truth and its acquaintance with the canons of literature."

"Surely you won't deny him a place as a litterateur . . ." was Forrester's comment.

"I'm denying him nothing. It's you I'm trying to deny. I want to deny you the confusion that is so rampant . . . I wonder just what you are getting out of this reading of yours. How much of Nietzsche's thought have you assimilated?"

"Really, I do not know, Father. I just know the man was a genius. . . ."

"Do you also know the man was mad?"

"But that was only late in life."

"Late in life . . . Hmph! You've been a farmer. Ever see full-blown plants without any roots?"

"Of course not. But what have they to do with Nietzsche?"

"Everything. Now, Alexie, I don't want to be anything like a wet blanket. Keep your enthusiasm for reading. Enhance it if you can. Reading makes the full man, as Bacon so wisely said. I'm all for it. I'm one hundred percent behind the idea of a man having a fully-rounded education. But nothing can be fully rounded unless it has a fixed center. In his *Idea of a University* Newman told us what no Catholic should ever need be told. Unless God be your center, Alexie, you will never have a fully-rounded education, nor will you ever be a fully-rounded man. I go further than Newman. I tell you that if God be not at the circumference, as well as at the center, and in all the area enclosed by that circumference, your education will be anything but fully rounded, and you will be 'off center' the rest of your life. Get me clearly: if Notre Dame does not make you and your buddies keenly God-conscious, it will not have made you rightly self-conscious; for it will not have made you conscious of what it means to be a man. We humans are beings who do not realize sufficiently how close we are to the Divine . . ."

"But isn't that very like what Nietzsche said. . . ."

"As like as night is to day — the finite to the infinite. When were you born anyhow?"

"In 1940."

"You are younger than I thought. You can have little memory of World War II, and none whatsoever of World War I. Yet, it can be said that Nietzsche spawned both those horrors. He generated Hitler even more surely than did Hitler's mother and father. He gave us that nightmare called Nazism — and all that followed on that hideous nightmare. You know little of those unbelievable horrors, Alexie. But I want you to believe me when I say that Nietzsche can be called 'the major seminal influence in the thought of the twentieth century' — and the explanation to much of the madness this century has witnessed."

When Forrester somewhat apologetically said he had found the man a thinker, I exploded with: "That's the trouble, Alexie. That's my whole point. For we are what our thoughts are. Assimilate the thought-patterns of Friedrich Wilhelm Nietzsche and all but unconsciously you'll cease to be Franz Alexus Forrester, the Catholic gentleman, and become that caricature of a man your hero named 'Superman.' "

"The translation I use calls it 'Overman.' Same idea. But, look here, Father, isn't that precisely what you Trappists are aiming to be? Isn't that what every Saint was? Superman or Overman? Only yesterday morning the Retreat Master gave us one of our best talks — I heard Nietzsche. . . ."

"You heard Nietzsche! . . ."

"Yes, Father Andrew talked of the necessity of dying to ourselves before we can become who we are. That's Nietzsche's doctrine of 'going under' . . ."

"You've *gone* under, Alexie, if you don't see that between our Saints and that German's 'Overman' there is the difference I just spoke about: not between night and day only, but between finite and infinite. Yes, between God and the devil."

He quieted at that and defensively said, "Oh, Father, I know the 'Overman' is no Saint. All I was trying to point out was that

Nietzsche had suggested the same means . . . There's some good in all writings, Father. I think I've found much in Nietzsche. . . ."

"I hope you found more in the Paschal Vigil," I countered. "That was writing in a language everyone can read, Alexie — the language of sign and symbol. What would your Nietzsche have to say about that ceremony? What have you got to say?"

"That ceremony moved me as much as, if not more than, Christmas Eve in Ireland. That *Lumen Christi* in the black of your big basilica was truly breathtaking."

"That's exactly what I had in mind, Alexie: that *Lumen Christi*. What would your man, who so boldly proclaimed that God is dead, have to say about that symbol of Christ's Resurrection?"

"God is dead? . . ."

"Aha! Just what do you know about Nietzsche's attitude toward Christ and Christianity?"

"Not too much. I know he says very little good about Christians. . . ."

"Did you know he called Christianity 'the one great curse of mankind; the one enormous and innermost perversion'?"

"I don't recall coming across that. . . ."

"Did you ever come across the passage that names Christianity — your Religion and mine, Alexie, the one Religion founded by God's Only Son — as 'the one immortal blemish of mankind'?"

I was stirred up by this time. When I saw the boy's eyes cloud with doubt or confusion, I launched out with: "Nietzsche would have sneered at the whole magnificent ceremony of last night, Alexie, from the flinting of the new fire outside the church under those stars and that brilliant Paschal moon, to the resounding 'Alleluia' at the end of the Mass. He would have laughed aloud at our renewal of Baptismal vows. He would have asked us to whom we were vowing. For he insisted that *God is dead*."

When I heard the youngster suck in his breath in shock and then say in a hushed voice: "God — dead . . ." I quieted somewhat and said, "I'm beginning to suspect you have not read enough of Nietzsche to know the man. That may be just as well. I'll get the passage about God being dead for you tomorrow. Tonight I just want to tell you that last night's ceremony would have shaken Nietzsche to his soul — or would have set him sneering. He had some foul ideas about History and 'eternal recurrence,' you know. To have looked upon the symbol of the Lord of History last night might have shaken the man. To see the monks, and the many laymen present, take fire, as it were, from Him who came to 'scatter fire upon the earth' might have affected your hero. But then again he might only sneer: 'Opiate!' Some 'opiate' that kept us wide awake all night, eh, Alexie?"

"Opiate?"

"Yes. Your great thinker thought the Christian Religion a drug, a soporific. The Reds, with all their high-geared propaganda about 'Religion being the opiate of the people,' were anything but original. Nietzsche claimed that to be fact years and years before Lenin ever got back to Russia. How much History did you see in the Paschal Vigil?"

"History? — I didn't even think of History."

That gave me my first chuckle in a long time. "You certainly need a well-rounded education, young man. And you need Christ as the center of that well-roundedness. When Christ rose from the dead, Alexie, He marked the midmost moment of time; He showed to all with eyes to see that History is very truly *'His-Story.'* I mean that literally. I insist that there is no such thing as 'secular history'; for I see all History as the evolution of God's eternal plan for mankind. To me, all History is truly Divine — or, if you will, Theandric; for Christ, in very truth, is the 'Lord of History.' He, as God-Made-Man, dominates every moment of time — even that before the Fall. . . ."

"Whoa, Father! Not so fast. Not so far. I thought Christ was born in time. . . ."

"He was — but before that birth in time He dominated every moment of time. But I see that neither you nor I will have time tonight to go into that. Tomorrow I'll open your ears as well as your eyes, I hope. Happy dreams. But none about Nietzsche or his 'Overman.' "

The next day I took Alexie for a walk. We had spent the

morning in his room chatting about his home and family. I was catching up on much that had transpired in Southern Rhodesia since the day I had heard his mother say with such finality: "They are not ready, Father. The natives are not ready. When they are, we will allow them to rule." Conviction rang in her voice; such conviction that I saw it would be bootless to argue. This Easter Monday Alexie filled me in with more facts that showed me just how his mother — and seemingly all the whites in the country — had arrived at their conviction. I accepted it as very reasonable. But I was also amused to note that young Alexie had not returned to his theme on Nietzsche's "Overman." But I had spent some thought-filled hours on the mind of today's college youth since first I had heard this college freshman touch on topics that filled the minds of men who had come from campuses which held no Golden Dome or had any Catholic Philosophy or Theology. I had concluded that the one crying need of the day was *clarity* obtained by *simplicity*. Hence, I had secretly decided to experiment with this exceptionally alert young man from Africa.

It was a magnificent spring day. Jonquils goldened the edge of a creek that plashed through a meadow, which seemed young and eager in its new green. The sky was a solid brilliant sapphire. The light breeze that blew reminded me of the psalms which speak of "skipping over the hills." These spring breezes seemed to be alive and frisking. Cardinals darted by like blobs of flying fire. Robins seemed to throw out their russet breasts as they came to a stiff halt after their quick, nervous run across the emerald tufts sprouting amid last summer's withered grasses.

Forrester showed his early training by noting every bird, every grass, and just about every tree. He asked not only the names of all birds and the few beasts we espied; but wanted to know all about their habits. I could do only an amateur's job in replying. Maybe it was consciousness of my inadequacy that had me quoting Francis Thompson as I pointed to a cluster of jonquils nodding in the breeze. "His fingers pushed them through the sod . . ." I said, adapting the lines from *Field-Flower*. "They came up all redolent of God." When I caught the look in Alexie's eyes at my mention of God I chuckled and said: "No need of Pupilometry with you around."

"Pupilometry?"

"That's what they call it. Scientist have a gadget now that measures the dilation and contraction of your pupils. They claim that, with these measurements, they can just about read your mind."

"Do you believe them?"

"There's something in it, Alexie. Cops have been using the idea for years on drivers they thought might be drunk. Our pupils react quickly to light and shadow. To fear and delight. To puzzlement and surety. Unquestionably, I just startled you by that bit of poetry. Your eyes just about popped."

"It wasn't the poetry itself, Father. It was the accent on the obvious — the place we supposedly clever ones never put it."

"Accent on the obvious?"

"How many of us ever credit God with that growth? How many of us ever think of Him as the shaper of that chalice and the artist who chose gold to top that green?"

This chance remark led me to recount how Frank Sheed had claimed that anyone who did not see God in a table did not see that table correctly. Had I wanted to avoid something very like a review of my Philosophy and Theology, I would never have made that remark. For Forrester took it up immediately and pushed me into deeper and deeper explanation of God and creation. I enjoyed it. I also found it work; for Alexie was anything but easily satisfied. I managed one hearty laugh, however, when in illustrating how others had clear vision of reality — which differs so much from mere realism — I had quoted Joseph Mary Plunkett's lines about

"I see His Blood upon the rose
And in the stars the glory of His eyes."

Alexie begged me to continue the poem. I did better. At least I thought I did; for I sang it for him to the melody one of my fellow monks had fashioned for me more than a quarter of a century earlier. Then the boy from Notre Dame asked me the author's name. I snapped out: "Joseph Mary Plunkett."

"The Blessed?" he asked.

"Your maternal Grandpa would hang you for that, Alexie. You've got your centuries, your plots, your patriotisms mixed up. But you've got the family straight. I believe Joseph Mary was a descendant in some line from Blessed Oliver. The man who wrote the poem I just sang, Alexie, more than likely was close friend to your mother's Dad. Plunkett was one of the planners of the Easter Uprising in 1916. He died for it. A martyr for his country just as Blessed Oliver was for his Religion. You should know the difference between Blessed Oliver Plunkett who died because of the Oates Plot and Joseph Mary Plunkett who died— shall I say — for *Sinn Fien?*"

"You're more Irish than my grandfather," said Alexie and started up the slope of the knob to which I had brought him.

I laughed at that for I find it most amusing that we, first generation of Irish immigrants, are so "patriotic" regarding a land that is not our native land — and so loyal to a people who are only remotely our people. It is a fact — and one that ought to interest Depth Psychologists, too many of whom can never find any real pure love or any genuine loyalty in the psyches into which they plunge. I laughed, too, because Alexie had given me the lead I had been looking for. I had come out this afternoon determined to show him a sure, safe way to Truth, Goodness, and Beauty — that of *simplicity*.

When we reached the top of the knob I sat down on the trunk of a fallen tree. Forrester took to the ground. Once he had lighted a cigarette I said I thought I noted a distinct difference in mental attitudes between those who had come from Fordham, George-town, Boston College, Holy Cross, Marquette, John Carroll, or Loyola, and those who had come from the Ivy League Colleges, Columbia, and State Universities. He nodded and commented that he would expect there to be a difference. But when I said that I found these Jesuit-trained men to think even a bit differently from men from other Catholic campuses, Alexie shifted in his posture and smoked a bit more intensely. When I went further and told him I thought that these men thought more clearly, more closely, more consecutively, more logically — and all because of the Scholastic Philosophy and training they received — he tossed his cigarette away and grasping his knees within his arms excitedly told me how it looked as if Scholasticism was on its "last legs," about to be "thrown out" — not only from Notre Dame, but from other Catholic Colleges as well.

This was news to me — and not good news! I told this young man from so far away what a very capable Harvard Professor of Education had told an assembly of Holy Cross students back in the twenties and thirties, and though fads and fashions in Education and Philosophizing may have changed much in the decades since, what he had to say then is true today; for truth does not change from day to day. I told Alexie how Professor L. G. Mercier had broken out in a veritable torrent of congratulations to the students of Holy Cross because they had a clear-cut and complete *course* in Philosophy — one that would give them a clear-cut *course* in life, if they would but live their Philosophy.

"What do you mean: 'Live Philosophy'?"

"Philosophy is not a mere speculative science, Alexie. It is one of the most practical! *We are what our thoughts are;* and our thoughts will spring from our Philosophy. Think of the France of 1790; of the Russia of today; of the Germany of the 1940's whenever you are tempted to ask: 'Live Philosophy?' Scholasticism is not something to know. It is something to live. Hence, it can never be looked upon as a purely speculative science, although it will always be rightly viewed as a science that allows for, and even demands, plenty of speculation."

Then he asked if I might not be prejudiced. I admitted it. I also claimed to be a little bit perceptive. I quoted Professor Mercier's words about thought on campuses which had a History of Philosophy but no real course or *cursus* in Philosophy, as being "chaotic, pitifully chaotic." "How can it be otherwise, Alexie?" I asked. "I marvel that it is not more chaotic. Youngsters are exposed to the thought of a hundred different men, and almost as many schools of thought, and are supposed to make their own choice about which school they will follow, or whose thought they will accept as true. Why so many end up as agnostics is no surprise to me. Just the opposite. And now you tell me that Catholic college campuses are going this way . . . ."

"Not to agnosticism, I hope, Father."

"Almost inescapable, Lex. History of Philosophy is not Philosophy. College boys are not sufficiently qualified to sift the chaff from the wheat. Eclecticism is bound to result. This is the most disturbing thing you have told me since your arrival. This is truly devilish. Talk about piling confusion on confusion! We avoid confusion, which is the very work of the Devil, by simplifying and unifying our knowledge and our entire lives."

Then was recounted the way we reviewed our Philosophy — and our Theology — when life was younger. I told Alexie we always claimed that no man knew his Philosophy or Theology unless he could reduce it to a shoe-string, a collar-button, or brass tacks. He smiled. "No joking," I said. "Take that blade of grass you've been chewing. Give me its four causes: Final, Formal, Material, and Efficient." He just stared. "Tell me where it belongs on the Porphyrian Tree. Show me how you can get a Universal idea from that single blade. Explain the whole genesis of an idea from looking on it. Start with that tiny thing and philosophize on it and about it until you end up — not in outer space, Alexie, but far beyond the furthest reach of outer space, up in the realms of utterly intangible metaphysics which will have you finally before the Throne of God and face to face with Him who is."

His face was a study as he mused aloud: "From grass to God . . ." His eyes narrowed, and it was obvious he was thinking.

"Yes," I said, "and whoever cannot go from that blade of grass to God is no Philosopher, no Theologian, and I dare say that he is no man."

"Whew!"

"Man is only man when he thinks. He thinks only when he thinks clearly, consistently, cogently, conclusively. In one word, man is man only when he's logical. The simplest logic will take any thinking man from that grass to the Creator of all grasses — God. If you had your full courses in Scholastic Philosophy I'd make you start with that single blade you've been chewing and have you course through Minor and Major Logic, onto Cosmology, Psychology, Ontology, Ethics, and Natural Theology. That would be reviewing your Philosophy. That would be thinking like a man. That would be philosophizing in the truest sense of that word; for it would be going to the ultimate causes in order to know what grass really is. Not to any Science Lab. But just staying out here in God's pure air and thinking. . . ." Then I added, "Or should I say listening?"

"Listening?"

"That blade of grass talks, Alexie. Remember my remark about those jonquils down below being 'redolent of God'? That was a quote from Francis Thompson's poem on a *Field Flower*. He heard that flower of the field talking to him. He claimed it was not only 'redolent of God,' but 'garrulous of the eyes of God,' and even 'musical of the mouth of God' and 'mystical with the mirth of God. . . .' "

Forrester seized on that last and objected, "That's poetry, not logic, Father. I've heard Thompson called a 'mystical poet.' I don't remember hearing him called a metaphysician. . . ."

"A man can be a mystic, Lexie, without being a real metaphysician. But of late years I've been wondering if a man can be a real metaphysician without being something of a mystic. Metaphysics takes you higher than astronauts fly. Transcendentals bring me face to face with God. I don't see how they can fail to bring every thinker to the same encounter. Reflection on 'being' is bound to lead to Him who more than once described and defined Himself as 'Being' by saying: 'I am who am' . . . That is why my 'Irish' rises whenever I hear anyone talk about the 'God of Philosophers' and claiming — or at least intimating — that He is not the same God as He who is the Object of our Theology. You'd really think these men had two Beings in mind: one 'The First Cause,' the other the 'God of Abraham, Isaac, and Jacob.' Their very pseudo-distinction — to keep from calling it a 'stupid distinction' — shows the need I was trying to point out, Alexie, for unifying all your knowledge. And I still say you can do that by simplifying. There's the beauty — and the strength — of Scholasticism. It teaches you not only how to analyze, but to synthesize after analysis — without having any 'extra parts' lying around after your synthesis at that."

When he smiled I added: "Let no one chop down the Porphyrian Tree, Alexie. It would be more disastrous than cutting the feet from under Atlas. Our world will not only shake, it will crumble when men cease to think *logically*. That adverb is more important than the verb. There is plenty of thinking going on. But how much of it is logical?"

He frowned at that so I told him how I had felt complimented by one who thought he was condemning me. It was a long story of a young priest, one of the *avant garde,* who had consulted me on several matters and was shocked to find me so fixed in principles. He had ended the last consultation by calling me "too logical." Then I resumed my point about thinking and logical thinking by telling Alexie how I had come to the conclusion that many with high intelligence quotients do not always manifest high intelligence — and that simply because they have not been trained to think as Scholasticism trains one to think. I made my point by telling him of young Tom from Northwestern — a lad with an IQ of over 140, but whose Logic would never win a mark of forty in a system with one hundred as perfection and sixty as passing. Tom had no time for Trappists at all. To him they were not only "squares," "creeps" and all the other slang terms, but "escapists," "schizoids," and "neurotics" as well. Tom had read much, but not too wisely, nor too well. Which was tragic, for the boy had a lively intellect and was consumed with curiosity.

"Did you convert him to your system of unification and simplification?" asked Alexie.

"To some extent," I replied. "For I set him doing what I want you to do now: listen to that Spire down there."

Forrester drew aside a low-hanging branch and looked down the slope of the knob, across the fields, emerald in their spring alfalfa, across the asphalt ribbon of road that ran into the valley and up the hillside on which the Abbey stood, and stared at the silver spire which stood out sharply against a sky of cloudless blue. After a moment he asked, "Listen?"

"That's what I said. It speaks, Alexie — to all who think logically." I then went on to assure him that I could start with that spire and do in Theology what I had told him could be done in Philosophy from the blade of grass. Every tract from that on "The Triune God" to that on "The Last Things" could be recalled and quite thoroughly reviewed as one looked and, as it were, listened to that silent spire. For it told not only about the living and the loving God, but also about how men were to live and love — in Eternity as well as in Time.

Forrester kept squinting at the spire as I spoke. When I paused he brought me back to the boy from Northwestern and his reaction to Trappists by the quiet question, "Did Tom hear what the spire was saying?"

"I believe he did, Lex — and I hope the first word he heard is still ringing in his ears."

"What was that?"

"The one I want you to hear — and hear clearly. Listen . . . Do you hear that spire speaking your oldest brother's name — and the name of your grandfather on your mother's side?"

"You mean 'Michael'?"

"I mean 'Michael.' That is what the spire is saying to all who have ears to hear."

"Michael . . . Michael who?"

I groaned in feigned disgust. Forrester could not have been sure whether the disgust was feigned or not. However he let the branch he had been holding swing back into position. He went over to a fallen oak that lay half-hidden in the undergrowth, lifted it, and brought it to the top of the mound to serve as a seat for himself. I marveled at his strength; for the trunk was not small and I know the weight of oak. Once he had seated himself he squinted at the spire again, then turned to face me fully and said: "Never forget I'm just a few weeks out of what you would call 'the Bush.' I've been away from the books for over six years, Father. So be patient with this intellectual prodigal. I'm back to 'my father's house' inasmuch as I'm trying to study once again. But now what's all this about 'Michael'? Is that spire really saying that to thinking men?"

"It is. And saying it with all the tremendous and transcendent meaning it had when first it was sounded."

"When was that?"

"Long before Rhodes ever went into Rhodesia. Long before Columbus discovered America. Long before . . . Alexie, that name was first sounded when Heaven saw battle and Hell came into being. Does that give you a clue?"

Forrester turned from me to look again at the spire. He stared for some time, then swung back to me and smiled as he said, "Not a glimmer, Father. Enlighten my ignorance. Unstop my ears. I want to learn. I want to hear."

"Good. I like your honesty, Lex. The Michael I speak of is Michael the Archangel. We Irish are fond of his name. But it is not Irish at all. It is Hebrew, which we render in Latin as *Quis ut Deus* — which means 'Who is like unto God.' That is the challenge Michael the Archangel flung at Lucifer when that Lightbearer, the brightest star in God's brilliant angelic creation, was rebelling against God. *Quis ut Deus* is precisely what that spire down there is shouting to all mankind. . . ."

"But all mankind is not rebelling. . . ."

"I'm not saying it is. Nor does that spire. Nor did Michael. *Quis ut Deus* had meaning for the loyal angels then, just as it has meaning for the loyal among men today. It means everything to me, Lexie. It means my very life. For it is not a question so much as an exclamation. *Quis ut Deus* admits no answer. No one is like unto God. No one is His equal — as Lucifer would have made himself in that original rebellion against God, and as so many stupid humans have tried to make themselves since Lucifer. God is the Great Alone; the Utterly Unique; the one True and Lone Transcendent. Michael, with his cry, gives you God's Name and God's Nature — So does that spire."

Alexie was quick with, "Michael's cry — yes. But that spire . . .?"

"It sentinels the Silent City of God, does it not?" He nodded. "But why should there be such a City? Why should it be silent?" When no answer came, I finally asked, "Why should any men become monks?"

A laugh that was tinged with embarrassment preceded Forrester's, "You tell me. I've been wondering about that ever since I arrived."

I was in my element now. Alexie could not have given me better lead. I would use it for all it was worth. Very slowly and quite musingly I said, "God once traced a First Commandment on stone . . ." There I stopped deliberately. I was looking away from the Monastery, staring into the trees atop the knob. But I did not miss the quick lift to Forrester's head, nor the quizzical glint in his eye as he watched me. When he saw I was not going on he mused aloud: "The First Commandment: I am the Lord, thy God . . ."

"Precisely! Man must keep first things first, Alexie, if he would ever have order in his life, or in his world. Yet, I wonder if that first of all Commandments cannot be called 'the Forgotten Commandment.' I wonder if it is not transgressed more than the rest of the Decalogue put together . . ."

"Oh, Father!" came the protest. "Idolatry is a thing of the past . . ."

"That's what you say, Alexie; for you think of images to Caesar and dropping incense into a burning brazier. You think of idols of stone and wood. You're thinking of what is forbidden by that Commandment. I'm thinking of what is commanded . . ."

"Thou shalt not have strange gods before Me . . ." he quoted.

"I know. I know. Idolatry is forbidden, Alexie. But don't you realize that adoration is commanded? That's why there is a City of God on earth. That is why it is silent. That's why men become monks. . . ."

"Adoration . . ." he said slowly. "I never thought of that . . ."

"Not enough do, Alexie. Yet it is the first and final end of man — every man; not only of those who become monks. That is what Michael meant with his cry: *'Quis ut Deus.'* That's what the silent spire says . . ."

"Men become monks to adore . . ."

"You seem to doubt it. Yet that is why you were born. That is why you came into this world. That is why you — and every other man — live. Don't look so surprised. You spoke of accenting the obvious this afternoon. That's really what I am doing now. But it was you who also remarked on how seldom we *do* accent the obvious. You're proving your point right now by your puzzlement over the First Commandment. . . ."

"I'm really not puzzled, Father. I guess I'm a bit ashamed. . . ."

"Don't be, Lexie. But listen to that spire and learn your life's work. For thirty years this has been my favorite theme and my favorite thesis. I've claimed the real work of Trappists is not what so many take it to be: penance for an unrepentant and and unrepenting world. That is only part of it — and it is very secondary. In fact, it would be practically impossible were it not for the primary. If God be not God, there is no such thing as sin. If there be no such thing as sin, where is the need for repentance? But to get back to my original thesis: Trappists are adorers . . . Do you know that you and your campus companions have changed my contention a bit. . . ."

"How's that?"

"For thirty years I've wanted men to hear 'God! God! God!' from that silent spire. I still want them to. But, the more I hear from you college men, the more I want modern man to hear that spire saying 'Satan' . . ."

"Satan?" said young Forrester.

"You're startled, eh? Good! Now tell me honestly: Do you really believe in the devil?"

His eyes widened in unbelief. Shocked by the implication in the query he allowed the tiniest note of indignation to sound in his reply: "Why, of course I do."

"Did you hear my question?" I asked. Then more softly said, "My question was: Do you *really* believe . . . Has your faith been such that you've been actually conscious of the devil as a person? He is that, you know."

"Gosh!" came the drawn out exclamation as Forrester rose from his log. "What a thought . . . ! Why is it that we so seldom think of the devil as a person? What kind of thoughts do we have about him . . .?"

"About *him* . . . ? His name is 'Legion,' Alexie. He is not one — nor one thousand. But don't you be embarrassed by the fact that you seldom have thought of devils as persons. That makes you just one in millions — not a devil." I chuckled as I realized how my words could be construed. "Just another human who fails to think humanly, which, as you know now, means thinking logically."

I then told young Forrester how I had seen a book entitled *The Devil Takes a Holiday,* and how I wish it were true. But I added that I knew Satan never took an hour off, let alone a day. I said I'd like to see several books written with titles like *How To Recognize The Devil* — or *The Devil Goes Incognito* — or *You, And Your Personal Devil.* I got that far when I heard: "Do I have a personal devil?" I was leading the boy down from the knob at this point and we were on a narrow path. I countered with, "Have you a personal guardian angel?"

"I've always thought so."

"Well, there are those who think each of us has a personal devil as well. Why not? If a good angel to guard us, why not a bad angel to tempt us?"

"Is this Theology, Father, or fantasy?"

We reached a level stretch where we could walk abreast before I answered. "I don't suppose you'll find the *Pastor Hermes* on your reading list, Alexie. . . ." I could not conquer the temptation to add: "Not on the list made out by the man who gave you Nietzsche." He grimaced. I went on, "But if you're curious enough about the matter, I suggest you go to your new Library and look up Migne's *Greek Patrology* . . ."

"I don't read Greek."

"It won't be in Greek. You'll find translations up there. Look up John Cassian's *Colloquies* in Migne. Then search out the one in which he quotes Pastor Hermes as saying: 'Every man has close to him two angels, the one the angel of holiness, the other the angel of perversion.' "

"Do I have to believe that?"

"You won't be a heretic if you don't. But I wonder how wise you'll be. Augustine of Hippo — remember him? He wrote *The City of God*. He was anything but a credulous fool. He is one of the Great Fathers of the Church — a great Doctor — and one of my favorite Saints. Well, his thesis was that the History of mankind is naught but the story of the incessant war between the two cities: that of God and that of Satan. Ignatius of Loyola was no idle dreamer . . ."

"Founder of the Jesuits?"

"Right. You've made his Exercises. He had you contemplating two armies, two standards, two leaders . . ."

"I remember."

"But did you realize that Ignatius was talking fact not fancy; that he was presenting an actual plan of battle and not presenting mere parable; that he was showing you reality as it is seldom seen? Did you ever know that it was because of that particular meditation that we used to say that magnificent prayer to 'Holy Michael the Archangel' asking him 'to defend us in the battle' — after every low Mass up until we got the new Liturgy?"

"No, I didn't realize."

"Leo XIII was prisoner in the Vatican when he made that meditation Ignatius has in his Exercises. Those were troubled times — as are all times — for the Church. Leo XIII saw that the battle Ignatius spoke of was then going on — and will go on so long as there are men on earth. So he wisely ordered that prayer to the one who had worsted Satan when time was young. Much as I like the new Liturgy, I was sorry to see that prayer go; for I believe we need it more today than in Leo's day. . . ."

We walked along in silence for a while, then Forrester asked, "Do we each have a personal devil — that is what I'd like to know. . . ."

I admitted that I, too, would really like to know. "But wouldn't it be prudent, Alexie, to live as if we did have a personal devil, just as it is to believe and live our belief in a personal Guardian Angel? Neither one is an Article of Faith, you know. But I speak to my Guardian Angel and call him by name — the name I gave him years and years ago. And if I am any judge of reality, he hears and answers me. Then Ignatius taught me to 'think with the Church. . . .' "

"But you just said the Church does not teach this as true. . . ."

"You're fast, Alexie. Sometimes too fast. I said the Church did not teach it as an Article of Faith. I did not say the Church did not teach it. In fact if you were really thinking, you'd see that, practically speaking, she does teach it. Think of Baptism. Whenever it is conferred there are exorcisms . . . We exorcise only the devil. Why did Mother Church ask you such direct questions at your Baptism. . . ."

"I don't remember my Baptism . . ."

"Neither do I remember mine. But what did you take the renewal of our Baptismal Vows to be, just last Saturday night, during the Paschal Vigil? Did you think we were putting on a show? Going through a mere formality? Holy Mother Church believes in sign and symbol but never in sheer insignificance. Would to God all could feel the fright I have felt at times when those very personal questions were fired at me: 'Do you renounce Satan . . . and all his works . . . and all his pomps?' " I took a deep breath here for I knew I was becoming a bit too incisive. And yet when I resumed I could not keep the edge from my voice.

"Look, Alexie," I said, "I take St. Paul to have been one of the toughest-minded men in all History. I love that man from Tarsus. He believed in Satan with all his soul, with all his fiery being. He believed in what I call a personal devil. He spoke of 'the thorn he had in his flesh — an angel of Satan to buffet him.' "

Forrester said, "I've never felt I had . . ."

That is as far as I allowed him to get. "You've been like the rest of men," I broke in. "You professed a belief in the devil, but as for practicing that belief. . . ."

"How in the world does one practice his belief in the devil?"

I turned to him with a loud laugh. "How does one practice his belief in the devil? By realizing what St. Peter realized; namely, that 'your adversary, the devil, like a roaring lion, prowls about looking for someone to devour.' That ought to ring a bell with you. You've seen lions on the prowl. . . ."

"I have. And I've heard them roar. . . ."

"Good. But don't miss the point. Peter is not stressing the roar. If anyone should know the devil does not roar, Peter is the one. He himself was 'sifted as wheat' by the soft words of a servant-maid. What Peter is stressing is the strength of the devil. Like the lion, he is king; — and in the jungle, which is the world, he rules. . . ."

"Rules our world?"

"Your disbelief points directly to what I wanted to point. Were I to ask you, where Satan is king today, I'm sure you'd say 'Hell.' Right?" The boy nodded. "You could even give me Scriptural reasons for that belief, Alexie. But there is another passage in Scripture which tells you what I want you to hear. Jesus Christ, Truth Incarnate, called Satan 'The prince of this world.' Hear that? . . . of *this* world." When I saw the boy ready to protest, I held up my hand to check him. "Don't get me wrong. I'm anything but Manichaean. I'll never allow anyone to think there are two equal principles: one the Fount of all Evil, the other the Fount of all Good, as some men have tried to teach almost from the beginning of the human race. No. There is only One God — One Absolute Ruler of all — One Source of all being. But there is a devil. He is the 'Father of lies.' He is a person. He has been 'a murderer from the beginning.' He is the leader in that crusade for confusion I've told you about. How he confuses mankind! He has an angelic intellect, Alexie; most likely the most brilliant of all angelic intellects — and, since he hates you and me, he pits that intellect against our puny ones day in and day out. Further, he *is* the 'Ruler of this World.' Christ said so. In space, the realm of Satan is our world. In time, his rule is right now."

After walking along in silence for some time after that, my visitor said softly, "Sometimes it seems so enticing to be Manichaean. Their doctrine seems to explain things so neatly — evil —mental and physical sufferings — disease — even moral suffering. Things get involved at times, Father. We get confused." I waited; for the boy seemed to be groping toward something; he seemed to be thinking aloud as if seeking clarity for himself rather than communication with me. I also sensed that he was talking in such a way that he might conceal rather then clarify. He had some idea he was hesitant to bring to the fore. So I sauntered along allowing him to talk away. "Things get messy not only in the world at large and in the State, but in the family — and in one's personal life. It would be so easy for us to blame it all on that Principle of Evil the Manichaeans excogitated. How much more satisfying to us that would be than to reconcile messy things with Divine Providence. Your talk about the devil being Prince of this world complicates matters in one way, even as it clarifies them in another. . . . I know there is but one God, Ruler of all, as you say. But I also know something of the modern world, and it makes sense to say Satan is its Prince, its Ruler. . . ."

That seemed as far as Alexie would go with his thought. I knew I could not leave it there. But I really did not want to plunge into the whole matter of what is called "The Mystery of Evil." I suppose I was really sparring for time and thought as I said, "The modern world, as you call it, is ended, Alexie. At least that is what Romano Guardini claims. Have you read him? No? Too bad. Tragic, in fact. Correct that mistake soon. Guardini and others claim that when you, or anyone else, speak of 'the modern world,' you are actually speaking of a world that is postmodern. Some even call our era 'the post-Christian era.' Literally, of course, there can be no such thing as a post-Christian era. This is *Annus Domini* — the year of Our Lord, Christ — just as every other year from now until the end of time will be. But no one will deny that we are living in an era of neo-paganism. In that sense I suppose we can call it 'post-Christian.' "

"I suppose we can," said Alexie musingly. "But I'm a bit be-wildered just now, Father. No, don't get me wrong. It's not the idea of the modern world being post-modern, or the Christian era being post-Christian. I think I have those ideas straight. But this thing on Satan being the 'Prince of this World.' . . . I'm stuck, Father; I know this is God's world, that He alone runs it, rules it, brought it into being, keeps it in being. Yet I know Christ did call Satan 'the Prince of this world' — and I can see that he has done much rotten work in the world. But . . ."

"Can it be that my Notre Dame freshman is confusing two things? When we speak of 'the world,' Alexie, we can mean the physical cosmos — God's wondrous creation. We can also mean 'wordliness' — which really is of man's making under the direction of the Devil. When Christ spoke of 'the world' He was not talking about the earth. He meant the ways of those we call 'worldlings' — those people who live as if there were no hereafter, live as if there were no God. Satan is not ruler of the physical universe. But of the 'atmosphere' that covers that universe — the maxims, the morals — or better, the lack of morals, the fleshy, sexy mores of the modern world — would you not say the Devil is master there?"

Forrester did not answer immediately. He was walking along with head down. We were almost at the end of the road that swings into the pasture from the main highway. Just as we were passing through the gate the clock in the spire rang out the hour — and cleared my mind for me. I saw I would have to return to my unification and simplification theme — and I would use the spire for it all. I stopped at the juncture of the roads, gestured toward the monastery, and said: "Answer that silver spire, Alexie. Who is like unto God?"

The frown faded from his forehead. His gaze swept to the spire. He smiled slightly as he said, "That's about the first easy question I have heard from you all day. I can really answer it. "No one is like unto God."

"That is not the answer Satan gave Michael when the Archangel first sounded that battle-cry. Nor is it the answer millions give today. What Lucifer said the day Hell came into being is what is being said in many parts of our world today — and making it so much like Hell." When I got only a quizzical look as comment I added, "And the cruel part of it is they do not even know they are being questioned. They do not hear what that spire says. They do not hear that challenging cry of 'Michael — Who is like unto God?' Talk about being duped . . . Did you ever hear of the mystical body of Anti-Christ?"

He repeated the phrase in such a shocked tone of voice that I had my answer. "That's what I mean by being duped, Alexie. That's what I mean by the devil going about *incognito.* You've heard about the Mystical Body of Jesus Christ. In it you and I are members. Now go along with the thought of Ignatius of Loyola, Augustine of Hippo, Saul of Tarsus, Simon-Peter, and John the Beloved; go along with the truth expressed by Christ Himself, and you will realize there is a mystical body of the Anti-Christ. In that, too, alas, we can be members. We will be if we don't listen to the silent spire. Job was right, 'Life on earth is a warfare.' Christ and Anti-Christ are battling for your soul and mine; warring to win you and me as members of their separate Mystical Bodies." I got that far when I found it necessary to stop in order to unlock the gate at the rear of the monastery. As I took out my keys I got a good look at Forrester's face. It was set not in unbelief so much as resentment of the idea I was explaining. I knew I had but a few minutes before Vespers. I also knew I had to convince this boy of a fact that was as evident to me — more evident — than the silver spire in the empty sky.

"I see you find it difficult to accept, Alexie. Well, tell me this: Is Communism human or Satanic?"

As he crossed into the Abbey grounds he shot out the monosyllable, "Both."

"Good. In replying that way you have actually proved my point. Just as Christ is the invisible Head of His Mystical Body, and we humans are His members, so Satan is the invisible head of that mystical body of his — and, alas, many humans are his members. See the parity, Alexie? The Mystical Body of Christ is visible in the Vatican and in all who are in union with it. The mystical body of Anti-Christ is just as visible in the Kremlin and in all who are in union with that. In replying as you did, you also proved another thesis of mine. . . ."

"What's that?"

"One day soon you will be studying a thesis about the *'mira propagatio;'* namely, the thesis on 'the wondrous and wide-spread propagation of the Faith of Christ,' and claiming that this speedy propagation is proof that the Christian Religion is super-natural in origin. It is a good proof. But, Alexie, how about the *'mira propagatio'* of the Communistic religion?"

"Religion?"

"That's what I called it. That's what it is. It has its bible, prophets, priests, devotees. But now follow my argument. If the speedy spread of the Catholic Church proves it supernatural in origin — and it does! — then, does not the far more speedy, and far wider spread of Atheistic Communism prove it preter-natural in origin? If Christ be the Founder and Head of one Mystical Body, is not Satan the founder and head of the other? Alexie, it took us three hundred years to climb out of the cate-combs. It has taken them less than half a hundred to dominate more than half the globe. . . ."

I recalled the day Lenin and Trotsky took over, and told my visitor that most of us took them and their regime about as seriously as Paul and his preaching had been taken by the Greeks in the Areopagus. I recounted some of the jokes that had been made about the Bolsheviki, and how we took it all as a laugh-ing matter.

"That was in 1917 and 1918, Alexie. But who would dare laugh at them in 1947 or 1948? Who would dare take them as a joke today? The Bolsheviki of 1917 are the Communists of this hour. And I insist that their survival, growth, surge to position and power was and is more than human. It was and is preter-natural. It was and is Satanic."

"You prove your thesis, Father. But is it not frightening? Would you consider Marx a member of Satan's mystical body?"

"Indeed I would. So was your man Nietzsche. So is many a man, and many a woman in your contemporary society. Duped undoubtedly. Unconscious of their identity as members of that mystical body. But members nevertheless. That's the diabolical part of it all: he does it all so slyly. He is indeed master of deceit. He goes about *incognito*. That is why I am so anxious to have people hear what the silent spire says. They need to be alerted to the fact Peter proclaimed: 'he goes about seeking whom he may devour.' He's devouring plenty, I fear. Believe me, Alexie, the devil is loose; and we are the ones who let him loose."

"We?"

"Yes, we. We did not make the right choice."

"What in the world are you talking about now? What choice did we make?"

"The wrong one. You are too young to know about it, but back in 1928 Pius XI gave mankind a choice. In his Encyclical on Reparation, *Miserentissimus Redemptor,* he first presented the alternative. A few years later he presented it again in his *Caritate Christi Compulsi.* He told us then that if we did not turn to prayer and penance God would let the devil loose. There was nothing new in this profer of a choice. Mother Mary had been making it for years on years. At her every appearance . . ."

"At the one at Fatima?"

"At Fatima as at Lourdes, La Salette, Pontmain. We've had over a century of warning. How many of us, even now, have turned to prayer and penance?"

"Well at least you Trappists have. That's your life, isn't it?"

"Our life is worship," I snapped. "And let me tell you neither Mother Mary nor Pius XI had only us Trappists in mind when they called for prayer and penance. They had you and all your fellow laymen as well as all Religious in mind. They had mankind really; for all mankind is involved. But how many listened? — Yet all have made their choice."

"Why do you say that?"

"Because so many things have happened not only here in America, but in your own Africa, in places all over the globe, that require Satan as the only satisfactory explanation. And he is no 'over-simplification,' believe me. Rather he is theological justification, if you know what I mean. I just gave you one example in Communism."

"Yes, but I have have heard that even in Russia itself, despite all the propaganda, persecution, and purges, there are believers today."

"I've heard it, too, Alexie. But what are those few compared to the masses? I read some frightening statistics the other day: only 18 percent of mankind on earth at present believe in God. Of that 18 percent how many really worship Him?"

As I was saying this the mellow toll of the large bell rolled out from the tower above us. "That's the Voice of God for me, Alexie. He's calling me to my one work. Under that spire which is speaking to you, I am going to sing my vesper hymn to the One Michael — what shall I say? — Defended? Seems strange to think of having to defend God. But facts are facts. What have I been doing all afternoon — all my life for that matter? We have just time to go to my office where I have those pages from your favorite ready for you. They will show you how too many are playing with fire this day, and not realizing the danger."

TWO · WRESTLING...WITH MORE THAN FLESH AND BLOOD

MY VESPER-SONG this Easter Monday afternoon was not without distraction. How could it be when the opening psalm, the one hundred and thirteenth, told of "the hills frisking like lambs?" Had I not just used the same figure as I was leading Alexie across our meadow toward the hills called knobs? It is a magnificent psalm commemorating the wonders God wrought as He led His Chosen People out of Egypt. This reference to the Exodus and the Passover should have put all of us in perfect frame of mind for this celebration of the real Passover. The typology is evident. The application, easy: our Moses — Christ — leads us through our Red Seas from out our Egypts, through our own arid deserts and toward our Promised Land. I suppose I did give some advertence to the appropriateness of the psalm for the season. I am not sure. But of this I am positive: the psalm caused me real advertence to the conversation of the afternoon. For David speaks of the transcendence of the One True God and the triviality of every idol. Above, or in the midst of the psalmody this Easter Monday afternoon, I heard young Forrester's voice saying: "Oh, Father, idolatry is a thing of the past."

Then it was that I saw what had been nagging me since Vespers began. I was dissatisfied with my performance of the afternoon. I had set out with one purpose and a very set plan. I was going to alert Alexie to the ease of simplifying and unifying life by the use of a single symbol. I was going to have him hear one word from our silent spire. That word was to have become the sun of his universe. It would burn with brilliance at all hours of his day and his night. It would keep his world from ever growing dark. It had done so for others. It had done so for myself. But today . . . I had begun well enough. The one word *Michael* had been sounded. But then I had wandered as I had never wandered before. I had used *Satan*. I could have introduced into Forrester's thinking the one thing I was trying to prevent: confusion. Why had I done it? Why had I wandered?

I did manage some recollection during the next three psalms. But as we sang the antiphon of the day: *Alleluia,* the nagging dissatisfaction with myself came back, and a new question arose: Why had I never used this as *the* word that comes from the silent spire? It would tell all I had the word *Michael* telling. It might even be more appropriate than the Archangel's name. For, as far as we can translate the word, it means: *Praise Yahweh.* And that had been the end-purpose I ever had in mind as I told people that the silent spire spoke. I always wanted to alert them not only to the existence of their God but to their existential need to praise Him. I had used the silent spire as symbol around which I arranged my arguments for my *apologia* for the Trappist way of life; and had always gone on to show that praise of God was not only my vocation but the vocation of every man alive. *Michael* — Who is like unto God — had served me well; but as the *Alleluia* rang out this Easter Monday afternoon, I wondered if the word *Alleluia* would not have served me better.

That question was the subject matter of prayerful consideration before supper this same Monday evening. The *apologia* I always made for the Trappist way of life had ever turned into an *apologia* for the one proper way of life for every human being even as, or rather because, it became an *apologia* for God. The three are linked in a union indissoluble as far as I can see. Since there is a God, He must be adored by man. To me it has always been as simple as that. Hence, the Trappist way of life — that of adoration — is the one way of life on earth that seems closest to the life of Heaven. We know God. We love Him. What else do they do in Heaven? What else is there to do for all Eternity? What else does God do? Is not this knowing and loving our explanation of the Trinity inasfar as we can explain It? Is it not the way God Himself has revealed the generation of the Son and the spiration of the Spirit?

I stopped there to ask myself if the one word *Michael* said all this to me, or was my concatenated thought-process the result of thirty years of contemplating the spire and thinking of all its silence said to me? As I tried to answer that question honestly I saw the aptness of the word *Alleluia* for me, and its slight ineptitude for others. Every man has the vocation, the duty, the strict obligation to adore God; the first and final end of every human being is to give God glory — to praise Him. But we do not all fulfill the purpose, attain that end, the same way. My vocation is special. I have a specific function to fulfill in the Mystical Body of Christ. As a cloistered contemplative I have been authentically deputed to the one task of becoming, as I called it years ago, burnt out incense. My days and nights, my years — almost every split-second of them, — have as their formal object: the direct worship of the Living God. I am the lips of the Mystical Christ in choir. I am the hands and feet, the heart, head and living breath; I am the animated instrument whom God the Son uses for His One Act of Love called the Redemptive Sacrifice. In me, through me, and with me, just as I "in Him, through Him, and with Him," offer to the Father the infinite praise, reparation, thanksgiving, and petition that are His due from mankind. That is my day: Mass and the Divine Office as Perfect Worship. That is my life: *Alleluia!* But of my fellowmen, who, save those few called to other cloisters, have like leisure to worship God thus directly? During the Easter season the major part of my every day is spent in this direct adoration. How adequately, then, it is summed up in *Alleluia*.

As I took apart that word and dwelt on its last syllable, translating it as *Yahweh,* I stood with Moses before the Burning Bush. What a revelation took place there in Madian as Moses pastured the sheep of his father-in-law. *"I am who am"* was what God said to the man who asked what was His Name. *"He who is"* is how Moses rendered it when he spoke to the people. The richness of the word sets one in awe. The density of it. The profundity. As I mentally gasped and gaped before the Beauty and Brilliance of the Being *Yahweh* this Easter Monday evening, it came to me that all my life I had been laboring not to show people that He IS, but rather WHO He is. That was the truth of it. Even this past afternoon I had meant to show Alexie not that God *is,* but rather Who God is. Then why was it that I had used *Michael* and not *Alleluia* as *the* word from the spire?

I got my answer when I recalled how I had wandered from my usual pattern and had Forrester hearing *Satan* instead of *Michael.* The milieu that is mine by Divine Providence and distinct vocation differs from the milieu in which the majority of men live, move, and have their being. Modern man needs to know that the living God is the God of all the living, but just as they will "never miss the water until the well runs dry," so they will never appreciate the love of the living God until they are made keenly aware of the hate of the one who would be like unto God and bring them to eternal death. The cry of the triumphant Archangel is better calculated to alert them to the liveliness of the devil and his enmity to the living God than the triumphant cry of Easter *Alleluia* might be.

This bit of reasoning gave me insight into the reason why I suddenly shifted from *Michael,* as the cry from the silent spire, to *Satan* this very afternoon. They are correlatives, in a very certain sense. To anyone who knows Scripture the first name practically connotes the second. But then I caught myself and asked if I was not rationalizing more than reasoning. Who in the modern world knows Scripture that well save those who need not hear what the silent spire says?

Here I almost chuckled for it seemed to me that Alexie, somehow or other, had led me into what could be called the contradiction of my life. For decades of years I had labored to make people *God-conscious*. In my correspondence, in my conversations, in all my writings this had been my one goal. It was something of a passion with me. To explain *why* would be to write an autobiography. That is not the purpose of this book. So I will only say I felt that I had found "the pearl of great price," I had stumbled upon the "treasure hidden in the field," I had been handed the key that opens all locks when I became *God-conscious*. That key I would pass on to all; that treasure I would share; that pearl I would have everyone own. This God-given *Open Sesame* to all that brings peace and happiness here below I would share with every man who breathes. Yet this very afternoon I had been working to make Alexie Devil-conscious.

I did smile broadly as I recalled my talk on the mystical body of Anti-Christ. For I am sure than many of my closest friends would open their eyes in wide surprise if they ever found me talking or writing on anything but the Mystical Body of Jesus Christ. Here again I had to pause in my reflections to thank God for this other great gift. God-consciousness, along with the realization of my part in the Mystical Body and the Reality that is, had been the systole and diastole of my spiritual life for thirty years. It had all been glorious. But now I was talking to a boy whom I wanted to know the same gloriousness I had come to know, and yet I talked to him about the mystical body of Satan.

But there I stopped and did some calculations. When I was born, in 1903, there were in Russia, I am told, just a handful, eighteen or twenty, Communists. In 1917, when the Kerensky Government was overthrown, there were some forty thousand Reds in the land. But that, too, was but a handful compared to the rest of the population. Today, not fully fifty years later, that forty thousand has grown to over forty-two million militant atheists. Forty percent of the human race is under the domination of the Reds. That is the largest number of people ever brought under the domination of one power in the history of mankind. At this moment atheistic Communism rules over the largest land mass ever under a single regime, and has subjugated more people than the sum-total of the believers in Christ, no matter what their Church or sect. I shook my head and told myself I was not wrong in naming this stupendous success something preternatural, something more than human. And I further told myself that my idea of the mystical body of Anti-Christ was not sheer fancy. Again the ideas of correlatives occured to me: just as Michael connotes Satan for those who think scripturally, so the Mystical Body of Christ connotes the mystical body of Anti-Christ to those who think theologically.

I reached that point in my musings when it suddenly struck me that the present-day Communists were worse than Nietzsche. He claimed God was dead — intimating, at least, that He had lived; but to the Reds, He is not only now non-existent, but never had existence. That is a worse blasphemy. From it everything else in their regime follows quite logically: without God, no real authority; without real authority, no law and order; without law and order, no genuine freedom; without genuine freedom, no true human life or living. To such people nothing is sacred; hence, nothing is truly human — for man is a sacred being. I shuddered as these truths seemed to grow out of one another. With God non-existent, the future life a myth, religion only a hoax, where can there be moral law? With no moral law why not lie, murder, rape, starve peoples, torture? Why not deceive? I was hearing *Satan! Satan! Satan!* as these thoughts tumbled down one after another. For as I had said this afternoon he was "a murderer from the beginning" and the "father of lies." I was not sorry that I had asked Alexie if he believed in the devil. I was not so dissatisfied with myself for having shifted to the word *Satan* as the one spoken by the spire. Modern man needs to hear that. . . . Then I thought of the Book of Job. . . .

G K. Chesterton had called this Book "one of the four pillars of the world." Anyone who has read it cannot doubt that it is one of the most majestic pieces of poetry ever given mankind. But to call it a "pillar of our world" is calling it more than poetry — and Chesterton was right. It is grand Theology just as it is majestic poetry. It alerts one to the fact that Satan is a person —

a powerful person; but always subject to the All-powerful Three-Personed God. Some people are baffled as to its purpose on their first reading of this marvelous story. But it is not so difficult to discern if one reflects. What Satan was doing, "standing among the sons of God on that certain day" mentioned in the opening of the Book, is a puzzle. But his work from there on is quite evident. Besides consoling us who are so often tempted, showing, as it does, that temptation can manifest our virtue and increase our merit, it further proves that Satan's powers are very limited and can be exercised only with the permission of God. But the Book is really a tribute not alone to Job's patience, humble submission, and unshakable faith; it is a magnificent tribute to the transcendence of God. Job, in his own way, says what Michael said when Satan was Lucifer: *Quis ut Deus* — Who is like unto God? The answer is the same, but even more clearly articulated as we see what we so often call Divine Providence to be nothing less than the Fatherly Love, Kindness, Wisdom, Goodness, and Justice of God.

As I knelt there in the Basilica thinking of Job, it suddenly dawned on me that I could use this Book to alert Alexie to literature as well as to life, to God as well as to Satan, to the liberty of the Children of Light as well as to the limitations of the Powers of Darkness. The author of this Book — who is really God — has told all the magnificent truths I hear from my silent spire — and has told them magnificently. And what comfort modern man can draw from the experiences of this "man in the land of Hus." Job can free from fear those who live in a cringing crouch because of the dread which is theirs — that annihilation may drop from the skies. For they should end the shrivelling of their existence when they learn to look upon the A-bomb and the H-bomb as God taught Job to look upon Behemoth and Leviathan. They were evil. They produced chaos. But they were ever under the control of the ever living, always loving God.

Before I arose from that prayerful consideration I had resolved to have Forrester read this Book as preparation for all I wanted him to hear from Gethsemani's silent spire. The final chapters would serve my purpose perfectly. For they show that God is creative Love; that He is ever at work in our universe; is aware of all that is going on; is constantly in control — not only of the forces of Nature, but also of the powers that we name preternatural. Better than all that, these chapters manifest this Transcendent One, this All-holy God, not only as living, but as loving His creature, man; — and as not only interested in him as a person, but ready to manifest Himself to him Personally. How I long for every man to be able to say what Job said at the last: "With the hearing of the ear I have heard Thee" — and — "My eye seeth Thee." That has been the ultimate aim of all my labors to get people to hear the silent spire. True *God-consciousness* is a constant awareness not only of Him who is Love, but of always being loved by Him. The Book of Job teaches that — and in lines that are truly lovely.

This last fact lifted my own spirits; for I was only too sensitive to the other fact, namely that what I had given Alexie before Vespers would make anything but uplifting reading. I wanted him to revel in the rhapsody of those lines that fall from the lips of God as He asks Job: "Where were you when I laid the foundations of the earth . . . On what were its bases sunk . . . Who laid its cornerstone when the morning stars sang together and the sons of God shouted for joy?" That is poetry. How sick what passes for poetry today looks when face to face with that! Alexie should delight in the warm radiance of the figures that flash forth line after line. "Who shut in the sea with doors when it burst forth from the womb; when I made clouds its garments and thick darkness its swaddling band . . . Have you entered into the springs of the sea, or walked in the recesses of the deep? . . . Where is the way to the dwelling of light, and where is the place of darkness . . ." To stand with Job in silence and be thus questioned by God is to renew our youth — in all youth's splendour. For who has not wondered about the dawn and the dark; about the sun, the moon, and the stars? Who has not asked himself whence came the winds and who dropped the dew?

Forrester should savor the splendor of the queries: "Have you entered the storehouses of the snow, or have you seen the storehouse of the hail. . . . has the rain a father . . . who has begotten the drops of the dew? From whose womb did the ice come forth, and who has given birth to the hoarfrost of heaven?"

Alexie could not miss the magnificence of such imagery, nor the tremendousness of the truths. A God who thus shows Himself to a man, and shares with him the vision of His own cosmic responsibilities; a God who confesses, as it were, to a man, the weight of His cares for the universe, is a God who not only lives — but who loves His creatures, especially His creature, man. The philosophical problem of evil might still remain unsolved for Forrester after reading Job, but most certainly there would be no question of the theological reality of the rapport between God and man.

The college student needed to hear Job say with sound sense: "I know that thou canst do all things, and that no purpose of thine can be thwarted." For the pages I had given him to read would have him hearing a mad man. Nietzsche in his *Die Frohliche Wissenschaft* has a passage which is said to have driven the author himself mad. That could very well be; for it is a passage that can chill the stoutest heart. It runs:

> Where is God, he [the madman] cried. I will tell you! We have killed Him — you and I! We are all of us His murderers! But how have we done it? How have we drunk the Ocean? Who gave us the sponge with which we have wiped away the horizon? What did we do when we detached this earth from its sun? Whither does it go now? Whither are we bound? Far from all the stars? Are we not hurtling downwards now in an endless fall? Backwards, sideways, forward, in all directions? Is there yet a summit and a base? Do we not wander through an infinite void? Can you feel the breath of infinite space? Is it cold no more? Does not night come yet darker still? Must we not light the lamps in the midst of day? Do you not hear the gravediggers laying God in the earth? Can you not smell God's rotting corpse — For gods also rot away! God is dead! Dead shall God remain!

The gigantic imagery in the first part of that passage might hold young Forrester's attention for a spell, but the blasphemy in the last two sentences would most certainly break that spell. Nietzsche had his madman go on:

We have killed Him. How shall we ever be consoled, we the vilest murderers of all? All that was most sacred and most powerful in the world has bled beneath our knives — who shall wash these blood-stains from our hands? What water will cleanse them? What feasts of expiation, what sacred games must we invent? Is not so great an act beyond our power? Must we not become gods ourselves, if only that we may appear worthy to have accomplished it? Never was so tremendous a deed done before, and all that come after us shall, thereby, belong to a history greater than all that has gone before.

Were Forrester my own age those last sentences might conjure up the face and figure of the little man History must call Hitler. Men competent to diagnose mental sickness have concluded that the Austrian house-painter was mad — as mad as Nietzsche's mad-man. But from what History has to tell of Adolph Hitler it is unlikely that he would have called for water to wash his hands or dream of sacred games and feasts of expiation. He more likely would say something like what Nietzsche has his madman say at the end:

Then the madman was silent and once again looked at those who were listening to him: they, too, were silent, and cast anxious glances upon him. Finally he hurled the lantern upon the ground and it was broken into fragments and the light was extinguished. "I have come too soon," he cried, "the time is not yet at hand. This tremendous event is still upon its way; it is drawing near, but it has not yet reached the ears of man. Lightning and thunder, the light of stars, great deeds, even after they are accomplished, all need time before they can be seen and heard. This deed is yet more distant from you than the remotest constellations — yet you have done it!

The passage fascinates me from many angles. I have often said to myself, after reading it, "Tho' this be madness, yet there is method in it." For I often think that many men have killed God, as far as they are concerned; yet, to them, the "deed is more distant than the remotest constellation." Consciences do atrophy!

As I was wrestling with the nagging sense of dissatisfaction throughout Vespers and my private prayer this theme of the death of God seemed something like a *lietmotiv* running through my thoughts. Ever since Alexie mentioned Nietzsche, the idea had been ever on the fringe of my consciousness. Of course it clashed violently with the dominant note of the season. Here we were in

Paschaltide, singing joyous *Alleluias* to Him who stands before mankind at this time of the year just as John saw him when this Apostle was in exile at Patmos, and says today what He said then: "Do not be afraid. I am the First and the Last and the Living One. I was dead, but how wonderful, I live forever and ever, and have the keys of death and of the nether world" (Ap 1:17, 18) — and yet I was wrestling with the depressing thought of those who claim that God is dead. I knew another depression, too, because of the memory of some young college men for whom it was too true that the ever living God, and God of all the living, was not alive!

Even as I went to supper this Easter Monday evening I found myself recalling Nietzsche's *Thus Spake Zarathustra,* wondering if my visitor would use the passage against me wherein Nietzsche tells how "When Zarathustra was alone, he said to his heart: 'Could it be possible! This old saint in the forest had not yet heard of it, that God is *dead!'* " A cloistered monk might look like "This old saint in the forest" to anyone just in from the teeming modern world. Well, I had heard about it — *too often!* It filled me with a pity — for God as well as for men. It fired me, too, with a longing to share the truth that it was all a lie! This is the truth that shall make men free.

Supper brought no cessation to my wrestlings. Why was it, I wondered, that men would rather listen to Friedrich Wilhelm Nietzsche than to the Trappist's silent spire — which really means listening to Jesus Christ, Truth Incarnate? Why? That they listened to the former is all too obvious. I had not told Alexie, but I was now telling myself, that here in America the German's mad thoughts had been assimilated too completely to keep some Americans sane. Only the past week I had read how the author of *The Noblest Cry: A History of The American Civil Liberties Union* had written that if paganism had been more intelligent, "the world would have been spared the two-thousand year sickness of Christianity." That is not only Nietzschean in flavor and form, it is Nietzschean in phrase. How that poor man needed to hear *"Michael"* — or is it *"Satan"* that he should hear?

Well, I would have Alexie read the Book of Job and I would insist that ultimately the lesson we humans are to take from it is the same we can learn from the spire. Job teaches us acceptance of God's will and an unswerving determination to "bless God" — that is, to praise Him. Atop the silent spire is the cross of Christ. The first recorded words of this Only Son of God become Man are those that tell of doing His Father's Will. The last recorded words are very similar. St. Paul tells us that this same Christ "at His entrance into the world says, 'Sacrifice and oblation you did not wish, but you have fitted together a body for me. You took no pleasure in burnt offerings and sin offerings. Then I said, "Here I am; I have come to do your will, O God," as it is written in the roll of the book' " (Heb 10:5–7). Life can be simplified and unified. as completely as that. Peter Howard did it by taking a phrase from the "Our Father" — and taking it seriously. In quiet moments of deep thought one wonders if there is anything else under the sun to be taken as seriously.

I left supper resolved to let my friend wrestle with Nietzsche's madman this night as I planned to do tomorrow what I had somewhat failed to do today: Have him hear one word from the silent spire, but have a veritable cascade of truths fall from that word; truths which would tell him not only who he was, but what he was to do, and, to some extent, even how to do it.

THREE · SEEING...WHAT IS REALLY THERE

I WAS in Alexie's room early but I found him up, dressed, and evidently at work on some notes. This was surprising, for I had told him I would call him for breakfast. "Well," said I, "we have an early riser. How did you sleep last night, young man?"

"Didn't. You kept me up."

"I?"

"Yes, you — you haunted me. I could not sleep with the thoughts you and your notes had given me. Nietzsche, with his very sane madman, sent me out under the stars. I saw your spire in the light of the Paschal moon. I heard it. . . ."

"Good. But why do you call Nietzsche's madman sane?"

"Father, that madman is most logical. Far more logical than many a man I have met who is considered sane. Your spire told me that. . . ."

This was something new to me. I had not thought of Nietzsche's madman as logical. I had never associated our spire with *Die Fröliche Wissenschaft* of the German scoffer. Though I had often thought that he might have been slyly playing on words and mocking our Gospel — our Good News — our Joy-filled Science or Knowledge — with his title which does allow for the translation of "Joyful Science" and "Cheering Knowledge" which might be rendered "Good News." I hesitated a moment, then asked: "How about some breakfast?"

"Had it early this morning — before you, I guess. I went down after the Vigils."

"Were you at the Vigils?"

"Couldn't sleep. Thought I'd see what you monks were doing at that ungodly hour. I saw. But I've been wondering ever since why you monks turn things so completely upside down. You rise when we are usually going to bed. You go to bed when we are just stepping out for the evening. Why? Seems to me you are not only going against nature; you are even going against God. He ordained sleep — and most of mankind takes it to be ordained that we sleep during the night hours. But you monks . . . Why, Father? Why? Don't tell me it is for God because I thought there was no such thing as time with God. He'd hear you during the day as well as during the night — and it would all be the same to Him, since there is no time with Him who is in Eternity. . . ."

I smiled. This was a new argument to me. This young man is fond of philosophical thinking, I saw — and yields himself to definitions a bit too readily. I sat on the edge of his bed, tossed a magazine he had left there toward his pillow, and asked: "Is it true to say 'there is no time with God' — or truer to say: 'There is all time with Him'? If they do not throw out Scholasticism up there at South Bend, Alexie, you'll learn that St. Thomas says something about '*Tota simul*' when he talks about Eternity. *All* time at once, is the idea. Of course that baffles our imaginations. But the endless, immeasurable NOW is the best we can do. So it is not 'no time' with God, but 'all time.' "

"But why get up a 2 a.m.?"

"Because you people haunt us. It is you who get us up in the dark . . . ."

"Come on, Father, tell me: just what is the idea?"

"You tell me just what you saw us doing last night — or more exactly, early this morning."

"I saw you singing your Office."

"Of course, but how 'stale, flat, and unprofitable' that sounds. Suppose I tell you we were racing the sun. . . ."

"At two-fifteen in the morning? Quite a head start you had."

"Do you realize, Alexie, that last night, — or this morning, whichever way you like to put it, — at that particular hour, you were among the very, very few people who were up praising God? Passionists and, I believe, Carmelites rise at midnight to sing their songs to Him. All other Religious rise early in the morning — five, half-past five, or six, to offer their prayers and praise. But in those darkest hours after midnight and before dawn the Trappists are about the only ones in the world who are up singing to Him who made both dark and dawn."

"But why?"

"Don't you think someone should be? Don't you think God merits it? Don't you think man owes it to Him?"

"At two-fifteen?"

"At every split-second of time. But what thrills me, Alexie, is that, thanks to the different latitudes in which our Monasteries lie, Gethsemani and her men race the sun clean across the Continent — and beat him."

"Race the sun?"

"That's what I said. We anticipate dawn from the Atlantic to the Pacific, singing praise to Him who set bounds to every sea. Our New York and Carolina foundations open the Trappist salvo to God on Eastern Time. We, despite the change made a few years back, really continue it on Central Time. Utah keeps it going on Mountain Time, and Vina completes it on Pacific Time. That has always thrilled me for I am one of those queer creatures who have a very keen sympathy for God."

"Sympathy for God?"

The lift to Forrester's voice and the look in his eye set me chuckling. "I see you agree with my brother, Father Jack. He has always found that idea of mine odd. Thinking as a Theologian he says: 'God cannot suffer. So, why sympathize with Him?' "

"Isn't that right?"

"I can't refute that logically. Can't even challenge it. Can't refute it, strictly speaking, theologically. But psychologically, and historically, or as they say today 'speaking incarnationally' — I hold myself perfectly justified . . . Have you ever thought, Alexie, about what a frightfully mean return God has received from His truly stupendous investment in creation — particularly from those creatures of His to whom He has given the most?"

Alexie threw himself back in his chair, put his two hands to his head, and exclaimed: "Easy, Father. Easy. Never forget I'm just out of the African bush. . . . Thoughts like that never once entered my head. But what is this about shocking return on lavish investment?"

"Some people accuse me of thinking of God too — anthropomorphically. . . ."

"Whew!"

"That's what I say, too, Alexie. And what a concept for them to have of me and my orthodoxy. How else should we think of God, especially since He became Man? Of course I say that *sensu aiente* and not *sensu negante,* as the Schoolmen always insist; for I well know that God is transcendent; Pure Spirit — *Actus Purissimus,* as Aquinas put it. But I also know this same transcendent God became Man, precisely that we men might become more and more like unto Him. Think with me on this level, Lex, and you'll see what I mean by poor return. . . . God created angels. Look what happened. I told you something of Satan yesterday . . ."

"You did. I heard Michael shouting 'Who is like unto God' as Satan rebelled."

"How that could happen, Alexie, has always been a mystery to me. You and I sin. But we have darkened intellects and weakened wills. We have three concupiscences — ever ready to burst into flame. We have a very decided inclination to evil. None of that excuses us, of course. But it does explain us somewhat. But look at Lucifer. . . . He had an intellect brighter than any sun; a will stronger than any steel. Think of all that is connoted by his very name: Light-bearer. How nearly he must have been like unto God who dwells in Light Inaccessible. Yet, Lucifer fell . . . 'fell like lightning,' says Christ. What a return that was to the God who had made him — and made him so lightsome. He took a third of the angelic host with him, Alexie. How that must have hurt God. . . ! Ingratitude hurts us. Don't you think it hurts God?"

"I . . . I really don't know, Father. I suppose it does."

"I'm speaking anthropomorphically, Lex — analogically. I know no other way for us poor humans to think of Him who is our Father. After that frightful bit of ingratitude, God created man. You know what happened almost immediately. That, too, is a mystery to me. How could Adam and Eve sin . . ."

"The devil . . ."

"Does that explain it? Have you ever thought how like unto God our First Parents were? They never existed in what you will learn to call 'the state of pure nature.' No. They actually never knew their own natural state. Peculiar thing to say. But it is true. God created them with all those preternatural gifts which raised them far above their natural state. Adam and Eve were immortal, impassible, and all but invulnerable when first created. They had intellects and wills which, compared to the brightest and strongest of ours, were like sun to candle flame and steel to straw. Yet, they sinned. Poor God! Angels first. Now, man."

"Why 'poor God'?"

"Look at the return. Do you know what creation is? No, you don't. Neither do I. Because we do not really know what it is to be nothing. Angels and men were called forth from nothingness. Men and angels were made 'Like unto God.' It's frightening. It sets one in awe — this thought of creation. Yet look what return God received. But I've only started . . . God closed Paradise after that horrendous act of ingratitude we callously call 'Original sin.' He did not create another Hell as He had for Satan. No, He promised a Savior! That, to me, is the most soul-shaking revelation of God that I know. Instead of having the earth open and swallow these humans who had so outraged Divinity, what does God do but promise that one day the earth would 'bud forth a Savior.' You know who that Savior is. His Only Son — true God of true God. Alexie, these truths shatter thought — stop all thinking — they demand adoration in awe . . . That promise should have kept Adam and Eve, Cain and Abel, all their children, and their children's children in a state . . . well, not of ecstacy maybe, but certainly in a state of loyalty — and great expectation. But look what happened. Read Genesis, thinking of 'return on investment' . . . What a sorry tale! Cain and Abel; the Deluge; Babel; Sodom and Gomorrha. . . . Read on: the history of Abraham, Isaac, and Jacob is not without flaw. Indeed no! But think of the history of the Chosen People under Moses. . . . What didn't God do for them: Egypt, the Red Sea, the desert. What did they do for God? After manna, quail, water from the rock. . . . Moses was so angry with them he smashed the Tables of the Law. Down went the Ten Commandments the Finger of God had written on stone. . . . But think on, Alexie: think of what we men have done with those Ten Commandments since Moses. . . . No wonder I say: Poor God. . . ."

"Again?"

"Yes, again, again, and again. The Chosen People were not exactly a grateful people. Read some of the names Christ gave to them: 'Stiff-necked' — 'Adulterous' — 'Murderers of the Prophets . . .' Yet, these were His Chosen People. Think of those forty years in the desert — and all they cost God: a Cloud by day — a Pillar of Fire by night — He fed them. He clothed them. He led them. . . . But, as St. Paul would say, 'with many of them God was not pleased.' How could He be? They were always murmuring, finding fault with this, that, and the other thing. Yet, He led them on — some He led into the Promised Land. But why delay way back there with the Patriarchs and Prophets? Look what happened when His Son came — when the promise of Paradise was fulfilled. . . . No room in the Inn . . . exile in Egypt . . . thirty years in Nazareth . . . then, as He 'went about doing good' in His Public Life, what was the reaction? — 'Winebibber — Glutton — Friend of sinners — Beelzebub — Devil!' Yes, the Chosen People of God called their Savior, who was God's Only Son, 'Devil.' . . . But that is not all. You've just celebrated The Great Week. You know how it all ended: God — on a Cross — between two thieves! And you wonder why I say: Poor God! You wonder why I am so filled with sympathy for God?"

Forrester reached over for his cigarettes and slowly lighted one. As he watched the smoke rise toward the ceiling he quietly said,

"I've never thought of things this way, Father. It is not a very pleasant story. . . ."

"Don't forget what we're doing, Lex: thinking about that 'return on investment' — and I've just begun my sad story. . . ."

"Just begun . . . Oh, Father . . . !"

"Want to look Reality full in the face? Want to see the texture of its skin? Well, realize that here we are today, two thousand years almost after that Death and Resurrection. Yes, two millenia, practically speaking, have passed since the first Easter, yet, tell me how this past Easter was celebrated over the face of the globe? You were here, Alexie — in what I call 'The Holy Land of America.' We had our Paschal Vigil. You participated. It was tremendous. Always is. Let's suppose, for the sake of argument, that the entire Catholic world celebrated it as intimately, as intensely, as Christ-consciously as we did here — what would that be as a return to the God who died . . . Alexie, have you ever juxtaposed those two words and studied them: God died! Look at them. Stare at them until you see them: God died. . . . Yesterday we used Nietzsche's phrase and spoke of God being dead. We knew it was nonsense. But this morning we are talking soundest Theological truth — reviewing unassailable historical fact: God died . . . Jesus Christ was, is, and ever will be, God. He was crucified on Calvary. At three o'clock on a Friday we now call Good, He died. . . . Have you noticed the legend on my Abbot's Coat-of-Arms? It says *Deus Crucifixus* — That means God died — Christ was crucified. I suspect that, like myself, he simply can't get over it. It sets your intellect reeling to think that God died . . . to think that men actually killed their God . . . to think that God so loved us ungrateful men that He stretched out His hands for nails — allowed His Heart to be emptied of its last drop of Blood. . . ."

I noticed that Forrester had sat forward, that he was looking to the floor, that his cigarette was burning away unsmoked. I realized that I had been meditating aloud rather than conversing, so I lowered the tone of my voice. As quietly as possible I said, "Yesterday I gave you those statistics about only eighteen percent of the human race believing in God. Yet, God died for us all, Alexie. There is not one who cannot say what Paul said about God and himself: 'He loved *me* and delivered Himself up for *me*.' Yes, He died out of a personal love for each of us as a person. Do you begin to see why I am so grateful to the men who founded this Order of mine; why I am so happy to rise in the middle of the night to lift my voice in praise of this God who died for us? Do you see why I feel so sorry for God? why I so often say: Poor God! — What a niggardly return He has received from His lavish investment in men!"

The boy arose at that. "You make out a strong case, Father," he said. "I have never had such ideas presented me this way before. You make out a strong case even for the Trappists. But now I have a difficulty that plagued me before I came down — and it still bothers me. It is not original. One of my classmates, when I told him I was coming down to Gethsemani, let loose with a scathing attack on you monks. I did not have a ready answer then and I really have no ready answer now. What you've just said tells me something. I see that you praise God. Yesterday you were arguing that all men were made to praise Him. True. But as my fellow student said, Christ commanded that we love our neighbor. Christ commissioned His Apostles to go forth and teach all nations. He never said anything about going into a cloister. He Himself never lived in one. My acquaintance summed you up as Un-American, un-Catholic, un-Christian. . . ." The boy looked at me almost defiantly. I know not whether he was afraid he had gone too far, was insulting me, or whether he was demanding a real refutation. It was an odd look on his face.

"Your college chum is not alone, Alexie. Nor is he original with that kind of talk. I've heard it for thirty years. Not only I, but all the Fathers in the recent Vatican Council heard very much the same. And not from a college boy, but from a fully consecrated bishop . . ."

Alexie's eyes opened wide. "You don't say . . ."

"I do say — and say it most emphatically. . . ."

"Well, what's the answer?"

"Over two thousand bishops answered this one one way. But I'll wager your college friend was tame compared to the way this bishop lashed out against men in the cloister. Of course I can understand his viewpoint. When a bishop needs priests for his diocese or mission, and has far too few and no immediate promise of more, then sees a place like Gethsemani with almost half a hundred priests, with, seemingly, no ministry — well, anyone can understand why he should raise the roof. One did in St. Peter's. The Press, of course, made capital out of it. But when the Decree on the Adaptation and Renewal of the Religious Life was published — over the Pope's signature, of course, and with the signatures of the Council Fathers following that of His Holiness, the Press was made to look foolish, as it so often was made to look; and the good bishop was made to look — well, to look for his priests any place but in the cloister."

"But what did the Council decree?"

"I'll get it for you today. I can't quote verbatim, but in substance it said Cloistered Contemplatives, men and women like us who live in silence and solitude devoted to God alone, have a high place in the Mystical Body of Christ — and added something like 'no matter how pressing the needs of the active apostolate may be' we are to stay in our cloisters praising God."

"Whew! That's strong . . ."

"And that is not the only place the Council spoke of us. In another it told how our manner of life should be preserved with care — 'utmost care' is how they put it, and even stipulated that 'the principal duty of monks is to offer a service to the divine majesty at once humble and noble within the walls of the monastery.' Does that help you?"

Alexie rubbed his chin thoughtfully. "Not exactly, Father," he finally said "It tells me nothing about the second commandment my friend stressed — good to our neighbor."

"Ooooh!" I exclaimed, and rose from the bed. "You've touched the tenderest spot in my whole make-up, Alexie. Sit down before I knock you down with my 'heresy.' . . . But first see if I cannot give you an answer for your friend up at school. . . . If I step on your toes, Alexie, is it your toes that cry out in pain?"

"Of course not. I cry out."

"But why? Why is it that your lips, which have not been touched, cry out in pain when your furthest extremity, your toes, are hurting?"

Forrester's forehead wrinkled in light frown. His eyes danced a bit in laughter. "What's the game?" he asked. "I suppose the the answer is that my lips and my toes are mine."

"Not precise enough. Once again I must say Scholasticism will give you the precision I seek. Don't let them throw it out on you. I'll sound learned, Alexie, and say: *'Actiones et passiones sunt suppositorum'* — which, in plain English, means, when you have a toothache, a headache, or a backache, it is not your back, your head, or your tooth that ache; it is YOU who ache in your tooth, head, or back. Yes, you the person. For you are the person who owns that body with all its various members. Your body has many members, Alexie; but it is one body — and it belongs to one person: Franz Alexus Forrester."

"All right. I own my body. My body has many members. When one is hurt, I am hurt. Is that it?"

"Again not quite good enough. Ah, there is nothing like Scholasticism for exact thought and precise expression. But let me stop kidding you with all this supposedly learned jargon, and give you something personal. Alexie," I said, and resumed my seat on his bed, "this is autobiographical, but only to show you the goodness and greatness of God — nothing about me. I'm going to tell you how God saved my vocation as a Trappist for me — and made all life and living look different to me. I'm going to tell you this personal marvel of God's love because it can change all life and living for you as it simplifies what seems so complex, clarifies what sometimes confuses. You have been working up in the hospital at South Bend, haven't you?"

"Um-hum. Needed some spending money."

"This example, then, should appeal to you as much as it appealed — and still appeals — to me. It will also enable you to answer your friend. Twenty-seven — no, twenty-eight years ago I ran across a word whose meaning I had to look up. That word was 'phagocyte' — Know what it means?"

"I'd have to look it up, too, Father."

"Well, I'll give you a lead, Alexie. Know what a leukocyte is?"

"A white corpuscle in the blood."

"Right. Well, phagocytes are leukocytes that have a very special and very important function. Suppose you cut your finger, and the cut becomes infected. Immediately, from all over your body, phagocytes will rush to the site of the infection, and there launch an all-out attack on the bacteria causing the infection." Alexie was all attention. But I did not catch the light I wanted to see in his eyes. "Think of that marvel," I said. "Some of those phagocytes might have been up in your brain; others down in your toes, when that finger of yours became infected. But, all unknown to you, they rush to your rescue." The boy simply shook his head in agreement, but still no wonder shone in his eyes.

I took up the magazine I had earlier tossed on his pillow, rolled it up, and brought it down on the palm of my hand as I went on with, "The day I discovered the meaning and function of phagocytes was my day of rescue, the day of my salvation." I leaned over and tapped Alexie's knee with the magazine. "That day my robe, with its whiteness, and my cloistered life, with its hiddenness, took on new meaning. From that day to this I have thought of us white-robed monks, whom the world hardly ever sees, or ever thinks about, as the phagocytes in the blood stream of the Mystical Body of Christ."

At last I saw the light I was looking for in Forrester's eyes. I sat back then and went on at a different tempo. "You saw us lined up in choir last night. I asked you what you thought we were doing. You answered: 'Saying your Office.' I told you then it was a flat reply. I tell you now, Alexie, that you were looking down on men who had risen at that ungodly hour to do all in their power to save the Body of God's Only Son. I say we 'Mystical Phagocytes' were rushing to the aid of sick members of Christ's Mystical Body just as really as phagocytes in your own body rush to the aid of any injured member in your body."

"Imagination helps, doesn't it?" broke in Alexie.

"Imagination nothing!" I snapped, and threw the magazine down on the bed in anything but feigned indignation. "I'm talking realities, Alexie. The Mystical Body of Jesus Christ is as real as your own body, as living, too! To me, to you, to any man who thinks, it is the reality of all realities."

"Touché! Touché!" exclaimed Forrester in a hushed voice. "Easy. I did not mean to contradict. I know it's a reality. But this concept of Trappists as phagocytes. . . ."

"Oh that . . . Excuse my outburst, Lex. But I get mad when anyone even hints that the Mystical Body is only a metaphor. Even the phagocytic concept need not be considered purely metaphorical. We are a unity 'in Christ Jesus,' you know. Why could it not be that my chant during the Vigils this morning sent a rush of phagocytes to do battle with someone like your college chum — and clear away that venom of his against cloistered contemplatives? Why could it not be that you were looking down on an entire Community of monks that was chewing away phagocytically at much corruption in certain members of Christ's Mystical Body this morning? Why could it not be . . ."

There was a bright twinkle in Forrester's eyes as he cut in with, "You never do use your imagination, do you, Father?"

What could I do? I joined his laugh and said what he had just said: "Touché. But now let me explain the Mystical Body scripturally, theologically, and without imagination. I'll stay with St. Paul for the most part. I'll end with Pius XII and his crystal clear Encyclical."

I was on my favorite theme now. Thanks to the talk we had had about Adam and Original Sin earlier in the morning, I could start with the parallel Paul draws in his Epistle to the Romans between Christ as the Second Adam, and the first man who was the head of the human race. Paul is convincingly clear. He contrasts Christ's obedience with Adam's disobedience; Christ's sanctity with Adam's sin; Christ's triumph over death with Adam's making death mankind's constant companion. No one can miss the unity of mankind under these two heads.

My next step was equally as easy. For all I had to do was take Alexie's own human soul as the principle of life, unity in his body, and identity. What his human soul does for his human body the Holy Spirit does for the Mystical Body of Christ — it animates, unifies, identifies.

Finally I went into the matter of the members, their different functions, but their marvelous dignity and identity. "We many are one," I ended. Then before Alexie could comment I added, "Now you have some idea of what we were doing in the dark this morning; some theological foundation and scriptural clarification for your classmate. I'll bet he is well acquainted with the word 'involvement.' It is one of those 'in' words at the moment. It is descriptive. Use it about us. Who could be more 'involved' — involved in and with the world — than we members of Christ's Mystical Body; even, and I may say, especially, we members who have left the world? Do you think that will clarify things for him?"

"I don't know, Father. Maybe if I can make it as clear as you have made it for me. You certainly make it personal and practical. . . ."

"Not I, Alexie. God made it that way. I simply try to make it clear. I long to make it vivid, vital — a matter of life and living for every human I know. It is a most consoling doctrine for me as a monk — and one that is most stimulating. It should be the same for everyone."

When Forrester turned and looked out the window with pensive gaze I gave out from memory the passage Pius XII penned in his Encyclical on the Mystical Body, which has meant so much to me — and to many others: "Deep mystery this," I quoted, "subject of inexhaustible meditation: that the salvation of many depends on the prayers and voluntary penances which the members of the Mystical Body of Jesus Christ offer for this intention." When Alexie turned from the window as I paused, I said very directly, "We members of Christ are not only our brothers' helpers, or our brothers' keepers, we are, in a very definite sense, our brothers' saviors."

Then my guest exclaimed, "And to think that my smart friend said you men ought to be out saving souls. . . ."

"We save souls, Alexie — plenty of them. But that is not our main purpose nor our immediate end. I've got another pet thesis on that matter, but I'm not giving it to you now. I'll wager we saved many a soul by those Vigils you attended last night. What would you say if I told you that you were like Martha and Mary as you knelt or sat in the gallery last night: you were outside the tomb of Lazarus."

His face lit up with a merry smile. "I'd say you were nuts . . . that you are a man of very vivid imagination . . . that you are romanticizing. . . ."

"Oh, yeah? Well let me tell you I am using my imagination and romanticizing about as much as Jesus Christ did the day He said to His Apostles: 'Our friend, Lazarus, sleeps.' Remember that?" The boy shook his head. I resumed, "You made some mention of Gilbert K. Chesterton yesterday. Know what he said after his Baptism?"

"Haven't the slightest idea . . ."

" 'My name is Lazarus — and I live!' You and I can say that not only after Baptism, but after every good Confession. All of us are Lazarus — in the tomb — when we sin mortally. Christ, and Christ alone, can bring us back to life. That's the 'encounter with Christ' the new Theologians are telling about — using new terms but telling no new truth."

"You don't seem to think much of all these things, do you?"

"I don't, Alexie, because they are not new. Back when Rome was falling, St. Augustine taught all that every Sacrament was not only instituted by, but administered by Christ. 'I baptize' he said, 'Christ baptizes.' St. Paul said the same equivalently. Yet some young men today think they have made a new discovery in Sacramental Theology. The same is true about a hundred and one other new discoveries by these so-called new Theologians. Who is there who knew anything about Theology who did not know that Christ, and Christ alone, can say: 'Lazarus, come forth!' as the priest raises his hand over a man in mortal sin —

and have that man rise from the dead, stagger out of the con-
fessional alive as was Lazarus when he staggered out of the tomb?"

Again that mischievous light danced in Forrester's eyes. "Did
I ever intimate that you have been gifted with an imagination, Father?"

"You most certainly did, young man. And I wish you were as
gifted. I'm trying to get you to see. . . . Picture these Gospel
scenes for yourself, Alexie, and not only the scenes will come to
life for you, but Christ will be the living God He is. . . . But come
on, let's get out of this tiny room; it's enough to give anyone
claustrophobia. I have permission to show you the house and
the grounds."

With that we left the Retreat House and, after a short visit to
Christ, a visit made from the visitor's gallery of the Chapel, we
headed across the garden which lies between the Gate House and
the main building of the monastery. Half way across I said, "I
never kneel in that gallery without recalling the hour of my
entrance. I had never seen a monastic church before. The floor
plan was something new for me. The long, high, narrow nave,
and the emptiness of the center of the church struck me as
strange. The first hour of the Divine Office I assisted at gave me
a feeling of awe — but also a feeling that I can only describe as
eerie. The monks down in the body of the church seemed to me
like men from another world."

Forrester stopped in mid-stride and exclaimed, "So I was not
alone!" Then he caught up to me. "I had seen monastic churches
before, Father. In Europe I visited more than one. But Gethsemani and its men impressed me as different. As you say, they
inspire awe — give one a feeling of eeriness. That's what I
felt at the Vigils last night. Let's sit here a moment, Father,
you've touched on something that brings back the experience I
had under this tree last night while all of you slept."

With that Alexie led me to a bench under a giant Ginkgo. It
is a magnificent specimen. Everyone who comes to Gethsemani
admires it. The fan-shaped leaves, so distinctly different from all
our native growths, not only delight the eye but give welcome

shade to the whole area under the tree. It is seldom that I go near it without the exclamation I now gave vent to: "Isn't it gorgeous — this Chinese Ginkgo!"

"Is that what it is? Yes, it is a beauty. But you should have seen it last night under that moon and those stars. I staggered out here. . . . Yes, that is the correct word, Father. I had just been reading that powerful passage you gave me from Nietzsche. It may not have intoxicated me, but it most certainly set me staggering. But first, Father, tell me: don't you admire the magnificence of Nietzsche's imagination in that passage? What a picture of the world he gives when men have killed God. How does it go? Something about drinking down the ocean, wiping away the horizon, separating the earth from the sun, then all of us falling frontwards, backwards, sideways, upwards, downwards . . . What a description! Then he has something about an infinite void, infinite dark, infinite cold. . . ."

As he paused with a far-away look in his eyes I said, "You certainly read the madman's lines . . ."

"Ah, that's the point, Father. How mad was that madman? He is most logical. . . ."

"You said that before, Alexie. What do you mean? I've heard this passage drove Nietzsche himself insane. Yet you find it logical . . ."

"Of course. Look, Father, I'm no theologian, but last night as I sat here looking at your spire up there and thinking of that passage, I saw how absolutely right the madman was. Maybe it was the spire that talked to me. Maybe . . . But anyhow, don't you see that if men ever do kill God the world would be just as the madman pictured it — no horizon, no center, no light, no warmth. That's what I mean by his logic. The madman did not say it, but it is there by implication: God makes the world go round; God keeps the world in its place; God gives us light . . . It's as logical as two and two make four. Remove the base from under that statue of Our Lady over there, and the statue will fall. The same way with the world. I understood last night, as I never understood before, just what the Irish mean when they say: 'God keep you in the hollow of His hand. . . .' " The boy paused there.

"My friend thought last night. Good. He even thought some strange but very true thoughts. Congratulations, Forrester. I never adverted to the logic in the madman's address. But it's there. You've set me wondering now. . . . That passage, you know, is taken from a work whose title has always intrigued me a bit; for it can be translated — slyly, I admit — but quite truly, as Good News, or Gospel. Nietzsche was capable of that kind of thing. And now that you have oriented me to the logic of things in this madman's speech, I'm wondering if Nietzsche did not steal his ideas from the Gospel. . . ."

Alexie just frowned, so I went on. "When Christ, who is God, actually died as Man, what happened? Wasn't the world made dark? Wasn't there a void? Mustn't it have been cold? And when the rocks were rent who would not have thought that the world was falling apart? And would not those who went down the hill from those three corpses have staggered as you did, and felt they were falling this way and that? It's just possible that your Nietzsche was more influenced by Christ and Christianity than he knew. Some Depth Psychologist ought to make a study of that. . . ."

"Sit down, Father, sit down before you have me reeling again. Nietzsche set me staggering, but you . . ."

I sat then but must confess that this possibility fascinated me. I might have further explored the thought had not my friend launched into an account of his night under the stars, staring at the spire from this same bench. He caught my full attention immediately as he quite poetically described the night-sky, saying that while African heavens may have a deeper blue to them, they did not have near as much silver as he had looked upon last night.

"And that spire!" he exclaimed. "Lone sentinel of the night. The moon made it magical, Father. Majestic. And that overarch of bright blue sky with stars that were more white than silver. Then the silence . . ." The boy broke off, but only to turn to me directly and say, "The longer I stared at that spire and the cross atop it, the more I felt that I was the lone, living human in this universe filled with silence and stars. It was a peculiar feeling — especially after reading that madman's speech. Maybe because of him the world seemed more wondrous than ever, the earth and sky more solid, this tree above us was more than shelter; it seemed like an understanding and comforting friend. I guess I was scared when I first came out here. I lit a cigarette and followed the rising smoke with my eyes. It was caught by these fan-like leaves at first, then snaked its way among them up, up, up until — instead of the thinning silver smoke my eyes were caught by that solid silver spire. Then the whole afternoon came back and I sat here thinking thoughts that too seldom are mine. I thought about Michael, Satan, God . . . I guess that's what you mean by listening to that spire and hearing it speak, isn't it, Father?"

I sat back before I answered, for this young man's description had touched me more deeply than I cared to show. I could see that God was using Gethsemani as I had seen Him use it so often these past thirty years. Souls come alive here. Souls deepen. Souls become keenly aware of Him who called them into being. "Well . . ." I said . . . "yes. That's about what I mean. There are several things I mean when I say the spire speaks. But last night you should have heard more than the spire speaking. When you were describing the stars a while back I could only think of King David. 'The heavens tell the glory of God,' he said. 'The firmament proclaims His craftmanship. Day to day pours out its utterance — Night to night hands down intelligence.' That's one of his psalms. He heard everything speaking, didn't he? In another of his songs he tells how wondrous he found God's Name in all the universe. 'When at your firmament, I gaze' he sang one time — 'Your finger's work — at moon, and stars, which You have poised in space — ah, what is man, that You should think of him; ah, what is mortal man, that You should care for him?' "
. . . I paused, thinking Alexie might comment. But nothing came from him so I did not know whether he was gripped by David's psalm or was looking through me at something he had thought last night. I went on quoting: " 'A little less than angels You created him; with dignity and glory you crowned him!' That's

us, Alexie, as David saw us. And he ended with this truth: 'You
gave him sway over all Your handiwork; all things You placed
beneath his feet . . .' That is the dignity and glory of man. And
that is one of the psalms you heard us singing last night. What
did you see as you gazed down on us from the gallery, Alexie?"

His grin puzzled me. It seemed more of an embarrassed grin.
"I was an exicted boy when I went in to Vigils, Father," he said.
"I had spent a long day yesterday filled with thoughts and thinking. Some of the thinking, and some of those thoughts were up-
setting. Then came the madman and his killing of God . . . Well,
after watching you men stand in two straight lines facing the altar,
then turn to face one another across the church, then sit and rise
in unison as the steady flow of the chant went from side to side . . .
Well, I was mesmerized — then, I guess, hypnotized — and finally
I fell asleep. At least I caught myself dozing . . ."

I chuckled at that confession. "Power of rhythm. I well understand. But the point I wanted you to get is that we all have two
sets of eyes — those we use under the light of reason, and those
we use under the light of faith. We can be looking on one and the
same thing — but, depending on what light we use, we see that
one same thing very differently. For instance, you could have
looked down on us last night and seen nothing but two groups
of men going through some sort of routine or ritual in a large,
peculiarly constructed church. But if you used another light and
looked a bit more sharply, you could have seen men of flesh and
blood, in this the mid-twentieth century, wrestling with angels
just as Jacob one time wrestled with an angel. But this time they
were angels from Hell. . . ."

"Not really . . ."

"Yes, very really. We were wrestling with Satan last night
Alexie; wrestling for the souls of men —some of whom are too
steeped in flesh and too soiled with blood." The boy was ready
to protest again so I hurried on. "It takes Faith. But Faith gives
you the keenest vision. You see reality as it really is. Satan is
real, Alexie. Christ faced him in the desert after His forty days
of fast. What can we Christians who do not fast enough expect —

that Satan will leave us alone? Christ also told of the unclean spirit who, when once driven from the man he had more or less possessed, returned with 'seven other spirits — *nequiores se* — worse than himself!' That's frightening enough. But Christ ended that narration with a prophecy: 'The same will happen to this wicked generation.' Now granted that Christ was addressing the Scribes and Pharisees of the first century when He made that prediction, nevertheless he is a wise man, a true realist, and soundly religious, who hears Christ saying the same thing about us of the twentieth century."

"You certainly believe in the devil, don't you, Father?" The remark was made as Alexie was tossing away his smoked-out cigarette, but it had a peculiar tone it. Not pitying exactly, and yet not confirmatory. It annoyed me a trifle.

"You bet I believe in the devil," I replied. "Would to God more moderns did! I believe that is one of the devil's most successful tactics: to get men to forget his existence. They don't formally deny it, they simply ignore it — to their own detriment, believe me! Have you ever read St. Paul's Epistle to the Ephesians?"

"I have those Epistles read to me, Father. They are now called 'The Liturgy of the Word'; they used to be called 'The Epistle of the Mass.' "

There was a slight flippancy about that remark. It sparked me to say, "That's tragic. Here you are at Notre Dame, getting what is called 'Catholic Higher Education,' and I find you reading Nietzsche with real enthusiasm, yet you have never read St. Paul. Good Heavens, what a distortion! I'd be willing to wager that neither you nor the majority of your companions in your English Literature class have ever read the Gospels. . . ."

"You mean right through — from beginning to end?"

"Is there any other way to read them? Isn't that how you read a novel, a romance, a short story?"

"That was clumsy on my part," said Forrester as he sat back and crossed his legs. "Am I supposed to sit down and read the Gospels the way I would read a romance or a novel?"

"You've answered my question, Alexie. I win my bet as far as you're concerned. I'd be willing to double that bet as far as the rest of your class is concerned — and win again. What you and they need is a course in the Great Books. . . ."

"But that's just what we have now. That's where I got Nietzsche. . . ."

"Is there a Great Book that is not Catholic?" I mused aloud. "I wonder. . . . No, I don't. I know. Yes, I know that to be Great it has to be Catholic. I use that word in both its meanings. No book that has not a Catholic or universal appeal can be considered Great; for universal — catholic — appeal is the fundamental requisite for all literature; for all art for that matter. I use Catholic with a capital, too, Alexie. For in the two Testaments, in the writings of the early Fathers and the Doctors of the Church we have Great Books. St. Paul's Epistles, of course, belong among every gathering of Great Books. The one to the Ephesians will not only tell you much about the Mystical Body we were discussing up in your room, but also about the wrestling we monks do every day and every night. He'll tell you who our opponents are. . . ."

"Come on, Father. St. Paul did not know any monks, let alone you Cistercians."

"We were founded in 1098. He died about 67. But truth is eternal; and we monks are true. I claim we were wrestling last night. Paul describes it this way: 'Our wrestling' — did you get that word, Mr. Forrester? — 'is not against flesh and blood, but against Principalities and Powers, against those that rule the world of darkness, the wicked spirits that belong to an order higher than ours.' Now are you beginning to see reality? Saul of Tarsus was no silly romanticist. No indeed. But then again, we must never forget that God is the Principal Author of these Epistles — and God certainly is a realist. Faith opens your eyes, Alexie. In his Epistle to the Hebrews Paul says, 'Faith is the proof of the realities which we do not see.' "

"Well, if I was supposed to see you monks wrestling with devils last night, my Faith is weak. I must be blind. . . . But how about going to see that cave you told me about? or the inside of the Monastery which you are renovating? Those are realities I can see without any Faith. . . ."

"Don't be too sure," I said as I arose. "Never forget what I told you yesterday about Frank Sheed. He said whoever sees anything without seeing God in it, does not see it. . . . But let's go." I led my friend into what we call "the Yard" — that part of the enclosure which we usually keep cloistered even to our male guests. It holds all our shops and other buildings such as Library, Farm Buildings, Metal House, Barn, and so forth. I merely pointed these out to Forrester and named them as we hurried down the road which split some pastures and corrals; for I wanted him to see the cave before I would be called to my next Office.

The horses, magnificent animals, all highly pedigreed, caught his eye. He would have stopped by the fence had I not said, "They are not ours, Alexie. We simply board them for some wealthy folk in the next state. Hurry. I have only time to show you the cave before the bell rings for Sext." We wasted no time as we skirted the bottom lands, though I could see young Forrester was eyeing them with keen interest. Soon I was leading him into the cave and he immediately poured forth a veritable torrent of questions. What was it for? Who hollowed it out? What kind of stone was it quarried from? How did they ever manage to get the ceiling so smooth and uniform? How long was it? When will it be put to use? And so on and so forth.

The way his eyes were darting about and the way questions came tumbling out over one another I saw he was thinking aloud rather than listening for replies. I decided to lead him on. I told him my Abbot had hired two professional drillers to tunnel their way into this huge outcrop of solid limestone which forms the east end of the wide plateau on which our monastic buildings stand, so that Gethsemani's Community might have a modern bomb shelter. Alexie accepted the statement without a question. No one could blame him; for this cave looks like an ideal shelter, running as it does into solid rock for at least one hundred and fifty feet, stretching thirty feet from wall to wall, and having a

ceiling a good fifteen feet from the floor. It could hold our entire
Community with ease. I then told Forrester that Fort Knox was
only thirty miles away, and a very likely target for attack, and
added that any bomb dropped as far away as Louisville would
affect Gethsemani, so we needed a good solid shelter. When he
nodded solemnly I almost laughed; but instead I went on teasing him.

"Don't you see, Alexie, what a magnificent example we monks
will make to the entire world of the care God takes of His own?
Don't you see what a shining proof of trust in Divine Providence
we will give by having this gigantic shelter right here on our
grounds? Every thinking man will see that God, in His Wisdom,
had His elements work for ages on ages just that this deposit of
limestone be formed here so that we Trappists of the atomic
era would have perfect protection? From the dawn of Time He
had us Trappists in mind; for us — His very own — He would
make special provision." In the dimness of the cave, I could not
be sure of the look on Alexie's face, but I felt he was swallowing
it all, so I shifted suddenly and said, "Of course you realize that
the good people in the small towns to the north, south, east and
west of us, are not God's people; do not come under His Providence; need not His protection. It is only us monks. . . ."

Forrester let out a hearty laugh. "I see, now, Father. Now tell
me truthfully what this cave is all about."

I told him then that some bright young monk got the idea
that he could produce a cheese similar to Roquefort by storing
our own products in this limestone cave for a curing period.
Alexie was chuckling as I led him out of the cave. "Some bomb
shelter!" he said.

The sunshine and warm April breeze were welcome after the
dampness and comparative dark of the cave. We had just fully
emerged when Alexie caught sight of two monks at the far side
of the field directly in front of us. They were drilling some seed
into the soil. "Now that's what I'd call 'wrestling with the devil,'
Father. I've farmed. I know. But you monks in choir last
night. . . ."

I doubled over with laughter at that remark.

"What's the joke?" the boy asked, surprised.

"I guess *I* am, young fellow. Or at least you're going to call me the cussedest, most cantankerous, and contrary Irishman you ever met."

"Why so?"

"You say you see two men wrestling with the devil over there. I say I see two monks working hand in hand with God. . . ."

"With God?" snapped Alexie. "Manalive, have you ever worked on a farm? If you have weeds — and I see that you do; if you have pests — I'm sure that you do; if you know droughts — and I suppose you do — then you ought to know what I mean by 'wrestling with the devil. . . .' "

"I've worked on this farm for thirty years, young man," I said with a smile. "I've worked under a Kentucky sun as hot, I'll bet, as any that ever shone on Rhodesia. I've worked on corn, hay, soy beans, alfalfa right here in this field — worked until I was dog-tired and ready to drop. I've fought the pests you tell about. I've battled weeds. I've seen droughts. I've been a farmer. But do you know my definition of a farmer — at least of a Trappist farmer?"

"What?"

"A man who helps God; a man who helps God work out His Providence; a man who enables God to live up to His Name of Provider; a man who works hand in hand with Divinity that humans may know a harvest. God actually needs those two monks over there, Alexie, if He is to have a growth in this field this year. That's reality. That is why I call a farmer 'God's collaborator.' Do you like the definition?"

"Ye-e-s, I like it. But yet something seems wrong. What is it?"

I walked along for a while without answering. I was nonplussed at the moment. Usually men who have tilled the soil welcomed the definition I had just given — and welcomed it with enthusiasm. What was bothering Forrester? I hesitated before I finally said, "Maybe it's with your Theology of Work."

"Theology of Work?" he echoed.

"That's what I said. There is such a thing, you know. We hear plenty about the philosophy of this and the philosophy of that; but not near enough about the theology of this, that, and the other thing. We are not God-conscious enough, Alexie. That's why we are not the happy people we should be — and the happy people He wants us to be. God made us to be happy — not only in the hereafter, but very especially in the here and now. We can be, we will be, if we think theologically. Maybe your difficulty lies in the fact that sin changed work into labor."

The boy frowned. "There's a difference, Alexie. Mighty difference. Sin brought forth those weeds you talked about — and those pests you mentioned. Sin sowed the thorns and thistles that plague every farmer — just as God promised they would plague us. Sin made farming labor. But you and I can make it simply work. Work, you see, was not a punishment laid on man because of sin. Oh, no. Far from it. Work is a dignity given man by God. Before the Serpent got Eve's ear, Adam worked. In fact Genesis tells us explicitly that God placed Adam in the Garden precisely as a workman. Adam was to 'dress it and keep it.' You ought to read Genesis, Alexie. It's a very interesting, and very enlightening book. You can get your theology on work from it. You will learn that work is a pleasure — and always would have been had Adam not sinned." We were just abreast a small lake we had made in a hollow above the bottom lands as I said this. The lake gave me an example. "There is what I mean by collaborating with God. He sent the rains. We stored them up so that the fields down below will never know real drought. It is the old story St. Paul told: We plant. We and God water. He gives the increase. We gather it in." When I saw the young man's head nod in understanding, I started up the road again and said, "It's thrilling to realize you are part and parcel of Divine Providence; that you are working hand in hand with God. Could any man ask for greater dignity? Philosophy or Sociology might look down on dirt farmers and speak of them not without disparagement. But Theology can only call them 'the extension of God's own hands; His collaborators; His special agents for the working out

of His Providence.' Which would you prefer as more exact science;
Philosophy or Theology?"

"No question there, Father. But it takes Faith . . ."

"It takes mindfulness or memory. Do you remember that Christ
called His Father a Farmer once?"

"No!"

"Yes! *Pater meus Agricola est* — is the Latin. 'My Father is
the Farmer' is the exact translation. That comes in the passage
wherein Christ was describing you and me. He said He Himself
was the Vine — you and I the branches — and His Father the
Farmer who trimmed those branches — just that we might bear
more fruit. That's why I am so happy to be a farmer. . . ."

"You, a farmer. I thought you were a priest — a writer . . ."

"Writers get cramps, I hear. Did you ever see any writer get
callouses like these?" I held out my palms. "I farm much
more than I write, young man; for farming is really more my
vocation. You see, we monks are supposed to be self-supporting.
The farm is supposed to be the source of income. It is now. But
it took us, here at Gethsemani, almost a century to make it profitable. Gethsemani Farms are famous the country over today.
But who can estimate the cost in sweat and muscle, and real toil?
The soil in this part of Kentucky is anything but rich. Up in
what they call 'The Blue Grass' of course, things are different.
But here in Nelson County it has been a matter of dung, plow,
disc, and dung again; then dung, plow, disc, and dung again —
and that for over a century. We farm scientifically now, and our
soils have been highly enriched. But to get to the point I want
to make: We Trappists are not only supposed to be farmers, but
farmers who are contemplatives. Now how can that seeming contradiction be resolved? Can the man who labors, as we here in
Gethsemani have had to labor, know the leisure which is an
absolute *sine qua non* for real contemplation? Then, can the contemplative find time enough to labor in such a way as to support
himself — without losing anything of his contemplative spirit?
Some problem, eh? The solution is easy. Our labor is our
leisure. . . .

"Don't forget my definition of a farmer. The monk who thinks theologically — and that is the only way he should think — realizes what he is actually doing as he toils away at farming: he is working hand in hand with God, his heart beating in union with the Sacred Heart, his mind one with the mind of Him who alone can 'give the increase.' Believe me when I say a monk in the fields can be as close to God as any monk in the Sanctuary if he will be a realist. He need not think of that trite — but true — verse about 'One is nearer God's Heart in the garden than anywhere else on earth.' He need only think of the verse I gave you a little while ago: *'Pater meus Agricola est'* — then he will know what he is actually doing: working as the extension of the loving Hands of Divine Providence. He can contemplate those Hands as he labors away at his farming — and thus labor will be leisure — and leisure that is all love."

"Hmmm," said young Forrester, "You've given me many things to think about. . . ."

Though the bell was sounding announcing Sext to be but fifteen minutes off, I stopped where we were and said, "Darn you, Alexie Forrester. You disrupt all my plans. I have been laboring for two days, almost, to give you one idea. I want to unify your life by simplifying it. I want to clarify all your thinking by giving you one ruling thought, and look what you lead me into: Nietzsche's logical madman, phagocytes in the Mystical Body of Christ, wrestling with the devil, working hand in hand with God. Listen to that bell. It is ringing out from that spire. What do you hear it saying?"

"Many things. . . ."

"Yes, too many things. And it's all my fault. I want you to hear one word: *Michael.* Well . . . I'll go in and sing to God, wrestle with the devil, and see if I can't come out with greater clarity for you. See you after dinner. Maybe I'll have an idea. . . ."

FOUR · PLEADING...TO BE ALLOWED
TO GO ON WORSHIPING

I WAS not too pleased with my morning's effort. It had been highly enjoyable; but I questioned how profitable it had been. I entered the cool cloister and headed for the church reflecting on the morning's walk and talk. I saw we had covered much ground; too much, maybe. But the fact that, actually, we had spoken of nothing but man's relationship to God, gave me some consolation; for as a priest of God my ever present and ever pressing duty is to bring God closer to men, and men ever closer to God; then as friend to this boy so far from home, it was not my duty so much as my joy to share with him the discovery I had made which is sure to lead any man and every man to happiness of heart, quiet contentment of spirit, and genuine *joie de vivre:* God-consciousness.

I was not far along the cloister before I suspected that my slight discontent with the morning's discussion stemmed from the fact that the plan I had made had never been executed. I had promised myself that I would simplify, clarify, and unify life for Alexie under a single sign, and sum it all up in a single word. The boy had allowed me no time for any of that. For, from the moment he had told me about finding Nietzsche's madman logical, and his own staying up practically all night to attend our

Vigils, he had led me on to discuss subject after subject that I had not planned to discuss. We had ranged from Eden before the Original Sin to atomic bomb shelters; from the wanderings of the Chosen People in the desert to scientific farming. But as I reflected, it slowly dawned on me that my main objective was being attained: Alexie was growing God-conscious. How else explain his night under the stars, his presence at Vigils, his persistent prodding into our Trappist way of life?

True, I had wandered far from the one word *Michael*, yet I had not ceased, for a single split-second, to talk about what I hear, and what I long for all other men to hear, in that one word which says *Quis ut Deus*. For me, Satan's sin, Adam's fall, God's promise of Christ, the fulfillment of that promise and the formation of His Mystical Body, man's dignity as member of that Body, his duty as branch on that Vine, the glory of being a Christian — and the responsibility to God and man stemming from that glory — are truths that cascade, as it were, from the one high source: the silent spire — and the word it speaks: *Michael*. I saw now that, though Alexie had led me on, I had not been led away from my prime purpose.

I was almost at the door of the Basilica by this time, and as I read the legend which arches it: *Venite, Adoremus,* I told myself that that is precisely what *Michael* means to me: "Come, let us adore!" I entered the door smiling; for I was telling myself that I was becoming a man of one idea. But before I reached my choir-stall I had consoled myself by concluding that, so long as *God* was that one idea, I was not doing so badly.

Just as Sext ended I remembered that I had promised to show Alexie the Decree of Vatican II on the Adaptation and Renewal of the Religious Life. I left the Basilica, hurried to the Scriptorium, and procured a copy of the Decree. Walking to my office I turned to Paragraph seven of that Decree and was happy to see that my quote of the morning had been substantially correct. The Council had stated: "Communities which are entirely dedicated to contemplation . . . retain at all times, no matter how pressing the needs of the active apostolate may be, an honorable place in the Mystical Body of Christ. . . ." That opening sentence of this paragraph was not as explicit about maintaining cloister as I had thought; but the final sentence of the same paragraph could hardly be more explicit. It ran: "Their withdrawal from the world . . . should be preserved with the utmost care."

In between those two sentences was a laudation of the cloistered contemplative life that would lift any monk's heart, and should effectively silence any critic who carped about our uselessness. The assembled Bishops had agreed and announced that our "apostolate is as effective as it is hidden"; that we are a "glory to the Church"; and "a well-spring of heavenly graces." What is more, they had stated that the "holiness" of the cloister not only "lends luster to the People of God," but adds "members" to that same People.

I wondered if Forrester's classmate would accept the conclusions of the world's Bishops concerning our effectiveness, or if he would, like so many others, cling stubbornly to his own opinion about monks being parasites.

I turned to Paragraph nine of this same Decree and there read something that appeals ever so much more directly to what I call the very marrow of my being. It says: "The principal duty of monks is to offer a service to the divine majesty. . . ." To me, of course, that "service" consists principally of the Sacrifice of the Altar and the Sacrifice of Praise from Choir. Mass and the Divine Office form one Sacrifice inasmuch as the Office is a setting, as it were, for the Mass of the day. This direct service of the ever living, always loving God is life and life's breath to me. Whenever I am asked about the duty incumbent on every mortal man of saving souls, I answer that such is the diastole of my heart-beat whose systole is always for God. Not everyone understands this kind of thinking or accepts that explanation. But, for me, who owns but one heart, the glory of God and the salvation of men form one steady throb.

Alexie's classmate came to mind again when I got that far in my thinking. I pictured him as a typical, alert, enterprising, practical, and quite pragmatic American college boy. He would not only want results, but would want to be able to see, feel, handle, and tabulate them. Truly American, I thought. But then I recalled the look on Forrester's face as he either defied me to refute this classmate of his, or begged me to give him some crushing reply. I wondered now if this Decree would satisfy even Alexie. He himself had objected when, in defending our way of life, I made no mention of saving souls. . . .

But then my memory clicked, as it so often does when "saving souls" is mentioned. For almost thirty years I have held a thesis which I know can be proved to the hilt, but which, I also know, some people would take to be "heretical." I have always held that if, *per impossibile* (and it *is* impossible!) a Trappist never saved a single soul, his way of life would be not only justifiable, but perfectly justified. That sounds strange to some. But it should never strike anyone as other than soundest Theology; for it is but saying in another way what has already been defined as a matter of faith; namely, that the *first,* and the *final,* purpose for any and every man brought into being is to *give glory to God.* That is what a Trappist does morning, noon, and night.

I got that far in my musing when I recalled the day I had attacked Giovanni Papini and, to my mind at least, completely refuted him. As I reached my office and sat into my desk I suddenly realized that I had been just about Alexie's age and in just about the same position scholastically when Giovanni Papini became something of a rage. His *Life of Christ* had been translated into English and had immediately become a best seller. It was frowned on, however, in some circles. I got a copy early — and read it not only with avidity, but with great admiration. For this man's explosive style appealed to me then as much as Leon Bloy's same style would appeal to me later. These men had color. They both were bold. Both were brave. Despite an exaggeration here and there, and some obvious errors, I liked both for what I considered their courageous sincerity.

It would be almost forty years later that I would meet Papini again. By this time I was in the cloister, and he had written things about the cloister that I felt should be refuted. Papini had published a book entitled *The Letters of Pope Celestine VI to All Mankind*. It was a brilliant work. Pope Celestine VI, of course, was purely mythical, Papini's creation. And the *Letters* were simply Papini's literary form for his castigations of everyone and everything — especially priests and cloistered religious. I saw much truth in what he said. I also saw much error. I finally decided to accept his creation and imitate his form by sending a *letter* of my own to *Pope Celestine VI*. I had enjoyed doing that composition. I sought out a copy of it now, thinking Alexie might enjoy it, and might even take it back to South Bend for that classmate to read. It took me a little while to find it; for, as my mother used to say, I "put things away too carefully." But find it I did. Then as I began to scan the first page I found myself smiling; for I saw that I had early adopted Papini's own style. I was flamboyant, if not flaming. I had written:

"Most Holy Father, Pope Celestine VI:

"I am a priest and a monk. Hence, Your Holiness addressed me twice, and every one of Your Holiness' lines stands out like trembling flame written on black velvet. How often I have asked myself the very questions you have put to all priests! And how often have I found them unanswerable. 'Do I believe in God?' You ask; '. . . in the living God who gives me life, who shed all the Blood in His veins, all the sweat of His Body, all the tears from His eyes, all the light of His words for the transformation of my life?'

"O, Most Holy Father, I want to say that I believe in Him with all my heart and soul, all my intellect and will, with every sinew and nerve in my body, with every last atom of marrow in my bones. I try to tell myself that I would not now be here at Gethsemani, locked in from the world and all its attractions by the five-ply lock of my solemn vows, if I did not so believe. But then Your truly strong statement comes to me: 'If every day when you held in your hands the very Body of the Divine Victim, your Faith were rekindled, you would not so often be distracted, so indifferent, so exhausted, so vague.' I am each of those things some time or other, Most Holy Father; sometimes I am all of them at once. That is why I dare not affirm that I believe with the burning Faith that I desire. Oh how tragically true it is that 'if we were as fire, all would approach to warm their heart. If we were intoxicated, all would sing with us the song of liberty — even in a fiery furnace!' But, Most Holy Father, I confess that 'my hands are not burning, my words are not afire, my eyes are not ablaze, and my face must have the wan pallor of one who lives underground.' I own it: as a priest, I am a disgrace to my God.

"If Your 'Letter to Priests' opened my eyes, what shall I say of Your 'Letter to Monks?' You wounded me to a depth I never knew existed in my shallow soul. I know my Order was born, as You say, 'of the impassioned will' of three Saints — Robert, Alberic, and Stephen. I know it was propagated by that incarnation of love for God called Bernard, and was for two hundred golden years 'the seed-bed of apostles, the womb of the wise, the nursery of the blessed.' But for me? You drew me to the life when you said that I 'like a bird who no longer flies, am content to rustle among papers and scratch among library books, to cluck in the church Choir and peck in the refectory.' I, who should be on 'indefatigable wing,' a 'gull wheeling in the open air,' an eagle looking straight into the sun, a swift ceaselessly circling 'the hid battlements of Eternity,' what am I? You say we should be the 'ravens of Elias, the eagles of St. John, the falcons of St. Francis, the pelicans of Christ.' I know we are like birds caged — and we do not even beat our wings against our cage's bars!

"You have shamed me to the center of my soul, Most Holy Father. And the torturing part of it is that I have no excuse to offer for my shame. Each excuse that leaps to my lips boomerangs on my honest heart. I cannot offer birth as palliative. Bernard was born of Adam, even as I. He, too, came from the womb of Eve. In his blood, as in mine, swam the seven germs of sin. Yet, he became a saint. I cannot blame enviroment. My Father, Benedict of Nursia, knew Rome when she was . . . a sewer of iniquity — even as is my own world. Yet, he became a saint. Assuredly, I cannot blame education. Twenty centuries of flame, struck by

God the Holy Spirit from the steel-sharp intellects of Fathers, and Doctors, and Writers of the Church, burning like signal fires on mountains that tower over a stygian world, have been mine. Stabbing into even denser darkness, into the Mystery of all mysteries — the Mind and Heart of God — have been those searchlight souls, the great Ascetics and Mystics; brothers of mine, my own fathers in this holy Order of Citeaux. I cannot even take refuge in that Scriptural quote, true though it be, that 'the Spirit breatheth where He will'; for Theology will quote back at me what is equally true: *'Facienti quod in se est, Deus non denegat gratiam!* And St. Paul, that mystic of mystics, confesses and does not deny he confesses: 'I am what I am by the *grace of God*': and Theology teaches that grace will never be wanting to me. Most Holy Father, I can blame no one but myself.

"You have asked: 'How many monks are there today who live lives of pure contemplation? Where are the anchorites of the first centuries; where are the penitents who tortured themselves to expiate the sensual pleasure of sin; where are the hermits consecrated to prayer and meditation; where are the mystics ravished with delight in God, united to Christ in His Passion, united to the Creator in a unitive vision?' And my only answer is: Where? — I really cannot tell, Most Holy Father; and that is the agony of agonies. We have in our hands all that Robert, Alberic, Stephen, and Bernard had. We have all that Benedict himself had. Gethsemani's grey cloister wall is no mere symbol in cement. It is a reality! It locks out the worldly world, and locks in men who would live with God alone. Not even Catholic magazines or newspapers come through that wall. And though the ether waves that break over it be filled with speech and song, no syllable of either ever reaches the ear of a Gethsemani monk. We are a world apart. We are alone. Why is it, then, that Your Holiness can still say that You do not 'perceive among us those ecstatic ones whose gaze is fixed solely on the blinding light of Paradise'? Why is it that You can still say that You 'do not know how many there are among us who plunge into the abyss of Divine Love in order to snatch forgiveness for sinners'? Why is it that You can write that condemnation and have it so condemningly true that 'if the heroes of action are few, rarer still are the heroes of contemplation'? May God forgive us our white-livered generosity, our venal bravery, and have mercy on our sloth!

"I have used the plural here and there, Most Holy Father; but I speak only of and for myself. Cistercian silence is a barrier before the souls of my brethren too high to scale, too thick to ram, too deep to mine. I know them not. But I have seen tall candles burning in the eyes of many, and I doubt not that it was kindled from the Pentecostal Flame. I watch some sink into the depths of prayer and can only anguish in envy and admiration. So the above is only *my* acquiescence to all Your Holiness wrote about me as a monk and a priest. I know our world 'is strewn with mountains of ashes, is a limitless hospital, one vast lunatic asylum.' I also know its one need: *Sanctity.*

"Oh, if only someone would run around America barefooted, as did the poor man from Assisi! If only someone would limp into our halls of learning, as did the wounded soldier from Loyola, and gather other Xaviers for modern Indies! If someone would only burn, as did that Saint of Clairvaux, and kindle in every state in the Union pyres for our mad, materialistic worldliness, then, phoenix-like, from those ashes, have arise strong-pinioned eagle-eyed soarers into the sun — men and women who would be saints! We need headlong lovers as were Francis, Ignatius, and Bernard. But, Most Holy Father, perhaps we need even more men and women like Teresa of Avila, John of the Cross, and the little Lily of Lisieux — *cloistered contemplatives!*

"Toward the close of Your 'Letter to Monks' You say: 'In this hour of imminent barbarity, charity is the paramount necessity.' Truer words never found way to print. We have seen charity grow cold, Most Holy Father. We have lamented our inability to rekindle it. With Your Holiness not a few of us have thought that we have heard the ominous pawing and neighing of the Horses of the Apocalypse. The hour is indeed imminent with barbarity. But when Your Holiness goes on to say: 'All else, even science, *even contemplation,* must be put aside . . .' then add: '. . . it will be a wonderful day for humanity when you leave your cloisters to journey over the highways of the world, to make the King of Kings Emperor of all human creatures,' we gasp, we groan, we fling ourselves at Your Holiness' feet, and we beg. . . .

"I am not Catherine of Siena, Most Holy Father. I have not been raised up by God to instruct Popes. I am but an insignificant monk in a tiny Order whose characteristic virtue is simplicity. I am ignorant even of the proper way to address You. Yet I make bold to ask Your Holiness to reflect on the fact that history *does* repeat itself — and often with much stronger accent. And I plead with You to prevent certain repetitions — by bringing about others. Here are the facts . . .

"In the early twelfth century it seemed as if my newly-born Order was about to die. A long sterility seemed indicative of an early demise. But then came Bernard — and Citeaux knew a fertility few Orders have known before or since. A slight echo of that is being heard in America today. After a century of barrenness, Our Lady of Gethsemani has been delivered of two daughters within the past five years, and, by the time You will have received this, she will have given birth to a third, and possibly, even a fourth; for there is high possibility that in her centenary year she may bring forth twins! In other parts of the world a similar fecundity is being experienced. It seems as if the Order of Citeaux — at least that branch of it known as the Strict Observance (popularly called 'Trappists') — is to know a veritable renaissance. I know this will rejoice Your Paternal heart even as did the incredible fertility of early Citeaux, the hearts of the then reigning Pontiffs. But, there precisely, is where history must not be allowed to repeat itself.

"In that same twelfth century a heresy broke out in the south of France which threatened to swamp the land, and render Christianity itself soft and soggy. It was called Albigensianism. It was nothing but the recrudescence of that hydra-headed thing called Manichaeism. But it gripped southern France in tentacles that closed and closed with ever tighter hold. Pope Eugene III sent Cardinal Alberic of Ostia as Legate from the Holy See who finally persuaded Bernard of Clairvaux to go to Languedoc and engage in personal combat with the heretics. Though Bernard's was the very Voice of Christ for all Europe at that time, his words had no lasting effects whatsoever; for that twelfth century was not dead — though Saint Bernard and Blessed Eugene III were — when the heresy broke out again with greater violence. Innocent III felt called upon to ask the King of France to use force. Thereafter history's pages are a horrible blur of human blood. Suffice it to name but Simon de Montfort to conjure up the crimson carnage. But, Most Holy Father, Innocent III also had Cistercians out in the midst of that melee; out of their monasteries; away from their quiet cloisters with their continual prayer and deep contemplation; out there in the world doing all they could by the power of their preaching to convert those heretics. The result? *Miserable failure!* Cistercian silence does not mother moving preachers. Solitude does not generate that *savoir-faire* so essential in dealing with those of this world. These contemplatives were hindrances rather than helps. But, had they been allowed to remain in their monasteries *to pray,* they would have accomplished marvels, as is evidenced by the uncontrovertible fact that, despite victory after victory by de Montfort and his troops, the heresy lived on, and even thrived until St. Dominic received, as pious tradition tells us, the revelation of the Rosary from Our Lady. Then things *changed!* For prayer, *omnipotent* prayer, had been added to the might of the soldiers' arms and the moving power of the preachers' words. The heresy was soon repressed, and gradually disappeared. Prayer proved of more avail than all the might of arms and armies.

"Do understand me, Most Holy Father. I am not of that extreme school which tries to maintain that prayer is everything. It is not! Both Simon de Montfort and St. Dominic were needed in that struggle: Simon to wield the sword, Dominic to sinew his arm by prayer. However, I am of that school which insists that arms without prayer, and even preaching without prayer, will prove ineffectual — and history bears me out.

"Think of Lepanto and Don John of Austria. Pope Pius V

saw that battle 'as in a mirror' from his chapel in far off Rome. He saw 'the last knight of Christendom break the battle line' and, for the first time in history, defeat the infidel at sea. But St. Pius saw more than Don John and his gallant men that morning. He saw Confraternities of the Rosary, the world over, *praying!* For it was Rosary Sunday, October 7, 1571. The saintly Pontiff commemorated that triumph rightly: by honoring John of Austria *and* Our Lady of Victory. For His Holiness commanded an annual celebration which we commemorate today on the first Sunday in October every year under the title of Our Lady of the Rosary, as St. Pius' successor, Gregory XIII, commanded. These Pontiffs knew what had strengthened the arms of the warriors — *prayer.*

"Think again of Vienna and John Sobieski. A little more than a century had passed since the victory of Lepanto, when the Ottoman was again at Europe's gate, pounding at the bastions of Christian civilization. But Christendom still had a soul of chivalry. On Sunday, September 12, 1683, John Sobieski served Mass, received Holy Communion, then with the cry: *'Non nobis, Domine, non nobis; sed Nomini Tuo da gloriam,'* led that immortal charge that broke forever the might of the Ottoman. Montaigne was right when he called Vienna 'one of the four most beautiful victories the sun ever shone upon.' But Innocent XI was even more right when he commemorated the victory by extending the Feast of the Most Holy Name of Mary to the universal Church; for he knew it was *prayer* to the Queen of Peace that had nerved Sobieski to the charge.

"You will remember that less than a lifetime later, Clement XI was taking pattern from his predecessors, and was thanking the proper person for another astounding victory over the infidel. On August 5, 1716, the Feast of Our Lady of Snows, Prince Eugene of Austria met the Turks at Peterwardein, and crushed them completely. But the Pontiff laid the standards taken by Eugene at the feet of Our Lady; for he had implored her help even before he had sent a legate to any of the courts of Europe. He knew that arms were essential. He knew something else equally, if not more, essential: *prayer!*

"Of course You may tell me the battering-ram and the battle-axe have long given place to the "sword of the spirit." I know that, Most Holy Father. But I also know that as the nineteenth century died, a great Pontiff, Leo XIII, showed us how to bring erring man back 'to the paths consecrated by the Blood of the God-Man and the tears of His Holy Mother.' It was by the use of *prayer*. His *Magnae Dei Matris* was a call to a Crusade. In it he repeated what he had stated so forcefully a year earlier in his Encyclical *Octobri Mense;* namely, that *'prayer* has always been the principal force of the Church,' — especially prayer to Mary by use of her Rosary.

"Leo XIII needed no special revelation to come to that conclusion. The simplest Christian cannot think otherwise when he hears Christ Himself command us to *'Pray* always'; sees Him with the busy, ever helpful Martha, and the silent, contemplative Mary, yet insisting that 'Mary has chosen the better part'; watches Him pray before working His most striking miracles; and learns that 'being in an agony He prayed the longer.' Then the least thoughtful of men cannot miss the timeliness of Christ's words to the Apostles baffled by their inability to cast out a certain devil. 'This kind,' said the Christ, 'is not cast out except by *prayer* and penance.' Don't You think, Most Holy Father, that our world is 'possessed' by just 'this kind' of devil?

"Pius XI thought so, and said so on more than one occasion. That is why in his Apostolic Constitution *Umbratilem* of July 8, 1924, he wrote: 'If ever it were needful that there be those in the Church who embrace the purely contemplative life, surely it is most expedient today. . . . It is impossible that these religious, keeping their Rule not only exactly but with real fervor, should not become and remain the powerful pleaders with Our Most Merciful God for all Christendom. . . . They who fulfill the duty of *prayer* and penance contribute *much more* to the increase of the Church and the welfare of mankind than those who labor in tilling the Master's field.'

"I know You may be tempted to point out to me that this particular Apostolic Constitution is naught but a Letter of Con-

gratulations to the Carthusians, and that in such a letter statements of this seemingly extravagant nature are to be expected.
But, Most Holy Father, if that argument should seem weak
because found in a letter of congratulations to contemplatives,
what shall we say when we find the same argument addressed to
Foreign Missionaries? On February 18, 1926, Pius XI, The Pope
of Catholic Action, wrote his *Rerum Ecclesiarum Gestarum* —
an Encyclical on the Foreign Missions. In it he says: 'Just as We
earnestly beg the Superiors General of such (Cloistered Contemplative) Orders that by the foundation of monasteries, their
stricter form of contemplative life may be introduced and widely
spread in missionary territories, so likewise, in season and out of
season, do We pray you, beloved sons, to interest yourselves
therein; for it is marvelous what measures of heavenly grace such
solitaries could call down upon your labors . . . it is perfectly
clear (from actual experience) that such contemplatives, keeping
unbroken the rule and spirit of their Founder, and *taking no part
in the active life,* can be daily no small help towards the success
of your apostolate.'

"An exhortation to obtain as *co-workers* men who would *'take no
part in the active life,'* and yet insist that they will be 'of no small
help daily,' will seem strange only to those unacquainted with
man's solidarity in the mystical body of Adam through sin, and
in the Mystical Body of Christ through Baptism, Faith, and
Obedience to His Vicar. It is that double solidarity, Most Holy
Father, that moves me to plead with all the force at my command, even as it led Pius XI to write his immortal Encyclical on
Reparation — *Miserentissimus Redemptor* — of May 8, 1928. That
is the one role we cloistered contemplatives can fulfill to perfection. We can be penitents for an unrepentant world. We can be
bondsmen and bailmen for our brothers who sin and atone not.
We can be health-giving leukocytes in a blood stream that needs
healthy corpuscles badly!

"But if there should be anyone who still questions the practicality of the contemplative life when atheistic Communism threatens
to engulf the world in its mad, materialistic conflagration, let them

read *Caritate Christi Compulsi* of May 3, 1932, and *Divini Redemptoris* of March 19, 1937. Pius XI was holding out to mankind the most potent weapons obtainable that they might be taken and used against atheistic Communism. In 1932 he said: 'In the face of this satanic hatred of religion . . . We would consider Ourselves wanting in Our Apostolic ministry if We did not point out to mankind those wonderful mysteries of light that *alone* contain the hidden strength to subjugate the unchained powers of darkness. . . . It seems to Us, Venerable Brethren . . . that the evils of our times can be averted *only* by means of *prayer and penance.*' In 1937, this great Pope was even more explicit. 'The evil that torments humanity today,' he wrote, 'can be conquered *only* be a world-wide crusade of *prayer and penance.* We especially ask Contemplative Orders, men and women, to redouble their prayers and sacrifices to obtain from Heaven efficacious aid for the Church in the present struggle.'

"Pius XI is dead. But Communism is not. Can the reason be that we did not join the crusade? The Vicar of Christ was not alone in this call. Christ's own Mother issued the same command. Our Lady of Fatima urged us to *prayer and penance* — and to nothing else! For thirty years that plea was left unheeded — if not actually unheard! But, finally, Pius XII came forth and consecrated the world to the Immaculate Heart of Mary. The step was slow. But it was not, and is not, too late even now; provided, of course, that we really *give ourselves* to *prayer and penance.* His Holiness, Pius XII, recognized this clearly. That is why his every Peace Message rang with the cry for more prayer and more penance. His Encyclical on St. Benedict of Nursia is one long eulogy on both. But, to me, his most convincing act was one in the description of which I will have to suppress a few names.

"In 1948 a Vicar Apostolic looked out on his mission field and found it 'white for the harvest.' He looked around at his workers, and found them few — very few! But then his eyes fell on a Trappist monastery in his Vicariate. There, within that cloister, were forty priests who did nothing but say Mass and sing Office. If he could get those forty, or even fifteen of those forty, out in his field, what a harvest he would garner! He approached the Trappist Abbot. He told him the agonizing truth: thousands of pagans out there were dying as pagans simply because of lack of priests. In open honesty he told the Abbot that if he did not get helpers, he would simply have to close his missions. The Abbot shook his head in ready and real sympathy, but said: 'I'd love to help you. But, as you well know, I am only a subordinate. Without word from my General or my General Chapter I dare not move — and I doubt very much that either of them would ever give me word to move.'

" 'If that is all that holds you back,' said the Vicar with evident relief, 'get ready to move; for I am on my way to Rome. I'll get word for you — not from your General nor from your General Chapter. I'll get it from His Holiness, the Pope.'

"He went to Rome. He saw Pius XII. He told His Holiness exactly what he had told the Trappist Abbot, and ended with the identical words: 'If I do not get helpers from that monastery, I will have to close my missions.'

"The Holy Father sighed deeply, then said: 'If that be the case, my son, close your missions. Those monks are not to leave their cloister. It is behind their walls that they are most effective — not elsewhere.'

"It is that short, but most penetrating, statement which recalls to me now, Most Holy Father, the most perfect *apologia* I ever heard for the cloistered contemplative life. It is contained in two brief sentences. They came from the lips of my late Abbot, Dom Mary Frederic Dunne. He would ask any antagonist of the contemplative life two short questions. They admitted of only one very brief answer. He would look kindly at the objectioner and ask softly: 'You believe in the efficacy of prayer, don't you?' When the person made the only possible reply — an affirmative one — Dom Frederic would smile and even more quietly ask: 'Then what is wrong with a *whole life of prayer?*'

"I know You believe in the efficacy of prayer, Most Holy Father. So I beg Your Holiness to leave us in our monasteries that we may lead a whole life of prayer. Leave us in our cloisters and to our contemplation. Leave these mortals of a few short years, these creatures of clay, their crosses of molten iron. Leave us burning, Most Holy Father, that we may burn on and on, until we burn out for Him, and for all those for whom He so willingly burnt Himself out. Do, I beg You, do leave us in the one milieu in which we can be truly efficacious for the glory of God and the salvation of our sin-sodden world. Leave us behind our cloistering walls.

"There is one argument more, Most Holy Father. It was written by God Himself on the plains of Raphidim and the hilltop nearby. Lest it be lost to posterity God the Holy Spirit sphered it in infallibility by having it written into the seventeenth chapter of the Book of Exodus. There it stands for all to read — and to learn how utterly essential for any victory is *prayer*.

"Amalec came to fight the Israelites. Moses told Josue to go out and fight against the enemy while he with Aaron and Hur retired to the neighboring hilltop. They mounted that hilltop not to observe the battle; not to direct the warring host; but to *pray!* It is God the Holy Spirit who tells us that 'when Moses lifted up his hands Israel overcame; but if he let them down a little Amalec overcame.' With that bit of God-given revelation before You, Most Holy Father, perhaps You will see that, instead of urging us out of our cloisters to do battle with the world, You should be sending other Aarons and Hurs into the cloister to support our prayer-weary hands. For then it will come to pass that, even as with Moses, our hands 'will not weary until sunset,' and other Josues will 'put Amalec and his people to flight.'

"Most Holy Father, my final — and, to me, overpowering and undeniable — plea is that Your Holiness *be good to God!* I mean just this: in a day when a large section of the world denies God His very existence; in a day when, what we long feared as 'the yellow peril' is actually upon us, and is showing itself to be Red rather than yellow, and to Religion and Religious is proving a deadly plague; at a time when the world, which was made to be a mirror of God's majesty, images only man's distorted features — cold with the cruelty of ugly hates, I beg You, do let God have some lovers who can devote their entire hearts, their entire lives, their entire loves directly, immediately, and exclusively to Him *alone!*

"Your Holiness' most humble son and servant,

"A Gethsemani Trappist Priest"

Before I had finished my reading of this old copy I saw that it fitted in perfectly with the drive I was making to show Alexie what I might call "the rights of God," hence, I decided to give it to him to read. I smiled to myself as I realized that what I had always taken to be an *apologia* for the Trappist way of life was, in reality, an *apologia* for God, His existence, and His due. As this thought took hold of me I saw further. For if God exists, man should be incense incarnate. My defense of the Trappist life was taking on a three-fold effectiveness. It showed man at his best. I was actually making an *apologia* for man. For could not I adapt Thompson's lines from *The Sere of the Leaf* and have them apply to every man as I once had adapted them for the men of Gethsemani? Is it not true that at death every man should be naught but "burnt out incense"?

I resolved to try my lines on Alexie. I jotted a hurried note saying:

"I'll see you after None. I'm busy after dinner. Before you read my Letter to His Holiness, Pope Celestine VI, see if these lines, which fit Trappists so perfectly, fit you? (You're some sort of an English Lit major, aren't you? I'm helping your Professors out.) Thompson wrote:

The heart, a censered fire whence fuming chants aspire,
    Is fed with oozéd gums of precious pain;
And unrest swings denser, denser, the fragrance from that censer
    With the heart-strings for its quivering chain. . . .

There is Prayer and Penance and ever-longing Love. That is the Trappist trinity. How about you? As for the Letter — know it is a reply to Giovanni Papini — the perfervid. I sang in his own strain. But has not Thompson put my plea, or at least the reason for my plea, in four magnificent lines? Keep your heart-fires burning. I'll be seeing you."

FIVE • WATCHING...THE DEVIL AT WORK

AFTER None I found Forrester seated under our Japanese lilac tree. As I approached he arose and asked, "Father, is there any chance of my laying my hands on a volume by Papini? What a a writer! Such passion. Such poetry. He's great!"

I smiled at this enthusiasm and began to tease. "Flatterer! Do you mean to say that I so completely refuted my rival that I stirred appreciation in you for him and his works? I never thought I was that good. I thank you, Mr. Forrester, that's quite a compliment."

"No, no, Father. You've got me wrong. I didn't mean it that way at all. You certainly proved your point . . . Your case is conclusive . . . What I meant to say was . . . Well . . . you know . . . the quotes you had used from Papini . . . Well, they . . . they . . ."

Embarrasment glistened in the boy's eyes. I smiled more broadly. "Go on," I urged. "They what?"

"Well, they . . . You know what I mean . . ."

"Yes, I believe I do," I said as I turned and started toward the Gate House. "But, come on, let's walk. This is too beautiful a day to just sit here under a tree."

"But, Father," Alexie protested as he caught up to me, "I did enjoy your article . . ."

"Yet, you prefer Papini."

"I didn't say that."

"Well, you should have," I cut in with a chuckle. "I do. He is by far the better writer."

We went through the little Book Shop in silence, and we were a bit down the tree bordered lane before Alexie took me up again with, "I *am* sincere when I say I enjoyed your article."

"So am I," I snapped back, "when I say I don't write to give people joy; I write to give people convictions. I am out to prove; not to please. I most certainly don't labor at refuting an author just to set my readers clamoring for his works. What did you get out of my article anyhow?"

"Much, Father. Much. . . . But I . . . Well, I'm sorry about that request for Papini."

I laughed at that. "Don't be, boy. He's great. I love him. But now tell me what you got out of the article. . . ."

"Gladly," came the relieved reply. "But will you first tell me where we are going?"

"I'm taking you where you can see God."

He uttered a feeble, "Oh," and walked along in silence.

"Well, what did you get out of it?" I asked again.

"Ever since I read it," he began, "I've been trying to decide which it was that struck me the more forcibly: your phrase: 'Be good to God,' or your surmise that our world is actually 'possessed by the devil. . . .'"

"You'd never think *this* world was possesssed, would you? Look at those trees, those fields in front of us, those flowers; listen to those birds above us; drink in that sunshine that is filtering down through these African gum trees. . . ."

"Is that what they are?"

"So I've heard. Make you feel homesick? No? Snap out of it, Alexie. Enjoy this day."

It was a magnificent mid-April afternoon. To me the whole world seemed young — as young as a child standing on a hill with a soft wind blowing through its hair and a golden sun washing its eager features set in a complexion as shiny as satin and as soft as silk. I was surprised when Alexie did not catch fire. The day was that kind. It would set lights dancing in the dullest eyes, and give spring to the slowest step. It had set me atingle, and also to teasing. My companion plodded along, seemingly immune to both.

I pointed to the Ladies' Guest House atop the hill and told him his mother had stayed there. He gave it a turn of his head and a single glance. Even at the dehydrator — which should have intrigued him after his years flue-curing tobacco in Africa — he was not rising to any bit of bait I threw out.

It was not until we were well along the road which arrows its way between two gracefully sloped and brilliantly green pastures that he dropped his embarrassed and abstracted air and showed some interest in his immediate surroundings. He asked about the grasses in the pastures and our method of nurturing them. I thought he was coming out of his mood, but we had only reached the heart-shaped lake which lies at the far end of the pasture when he was enveloped again in his abstracted air.

I was on the point of jolting him out of his state when he said a thing that made me break into delighted laughter.

"What's so funny?" he asked.

I could not answer immediately. His remark had stirred up such memories that it was a few moments before I could speak. Even then it was through chuckles that I began the explanation. "Alexie, I was almost silenced, sent to the Holy Office, excommunicated, or some such drastic measure for once writing what you have just said. When writing to my youngest brother, who was then dying of cancer, I gave some remark Pius XII had made in some audience or other and immediately added: 'You see, Charlie, the Pope agrees with me.' Of course I was only being flippant. But will you believe it: when I put that in a book for publication one of my Censors took me seriously. He actually thought I meant that remark to be taken literally. Now God knows I'm conceited. So do a lot of others. But both God and others know

I am not *that* conceited. My kid-brother got a kick out of it. But, believe me, I almost got kicked."

"You're kidding."

"I am not! Censorship in the Church is no joke, my boy. That is why I feel like the Hollywood movie-director who used to go around pulling out his hair saying: 'With four thousand and five hundred other ways of making a living, I have to go and become a movie-director!' I say: 'With at least four thousand and five hundred other ways of getting to Heaven, I have to go ahead and become a scribe!' But, tell me, where did you find Pope Celestine VI agreeing with me?"

"Not Celestine, Father, Pius."

"Which one, the eleventh or the twelfth?"

"Both, I believe. But certainly one of them said something very like what you have said more than once; namely, that the devil is loose."

We were now climbing the steep part of the hill on top of which stands the Fire Tower. At the base of the Tower, after getting my breath, I said, "I'm going to show you the Beauty of God in such a fashion now, Alexie, that you will forget the devil — and wonder how there can be any atheists in the world — especially in springtime."

With that I began the ascent of the Tower which rose almost one hundred feet from the top of the knob. Alexie followed. It was not until we were within the box-like structure atop the steel supports that I explained to my companion how similar towers topped knobs in surrounding counties and were manned by watchers who, thanks to a two-way radio, could communicate with one another about any smoke they saw rising from the woodlands. "In the early spring and in the fall — in fact, in any time of a long drought there is always danger of fire breaking out in these woods. This system helps to spot it early and get fire-fighters out to the spot. These towers have no doubt saved millions of dollars of timber. Just now, thanks to the spring rains, there is no need for any watchers. That is why you and I have it to ourselves this afternoon. Now take in that panorama and see why I exclaim: 'O God how beautiful You are!' "

"You?" repeated Alexie.

"You are seeing God," I whispered.

The boy looked out. The sun had passed the meridian only a short while before; hence, its golden light was falling almost directly down on greens of every hue. Alexie turned from north to east, then slowly to south and west. Knobs rolled in wave after wave all around the circuit save in one spot to the southwest where a gap opened the view into another county. It was some time before Forrester spoke. When he did, his voice was soft. "You're lucky, Father. You're really cloistered in by these hills, aren't you? They close out a world that is noisy and give you this unbelievable quiet." Then he actually exclaimed, "No one up in South Bend will believe me when I tell them I've been in such a world. They cannot believe such a world exists. Not here in America. Especially not in the middle of this tumultuous twentieth century. Yes, you're lucky!"

"I know it, Alexie. Sometimes as I stand here taking in the sweep of those knobs I seem to feel the very breath of God on my neck. Don't you realize that God is Beauty? Look down through those trees. Catch the sheen on the church's spire . . ."

Alexie leaned out the open window of the Tower and peered down through trees that screened the monastery somewhat from view.

"Hear the message of *Michael?*"

He drew back from the window. "No Father, no. Not on a day like this. I refuse to think of war in the midst of so much glorious green peace."

"But manalive, the message of Michael is not only of war — not even primarily of war. He battled once, it is true. That is why I call him 'The Irish Archangel.' But it is not those Irish traits of battle and belligerency our spire calls up, but rather that other Irish trait of flaming Faith. Maybe I've had you thinking too much about the devil. Let's go down. But tell me, what would you say if I now asked you to think about the devil's being dead?"

"Dead?"

"You had me thinking about God's being dead all day yesterday, didn't you? Well, today let me reverse the roles."

"But that's impossible. After all you've told me these past two days, and especially after just reading your Reply to Celestine VI, I can only realize the devil is very much alive. I believe you when you say he 'possesses the world' right now."

"Well your latest literary hero wants to set the devil free — not loose, mind you, but free."

"What in the world are you talking about?"

I was at the trap door when Forrester threw that question at me. I stopped there and said, "Papini recently came out with a theory that God is all too good and all too merciful to allow Satan to stay in Hell forever. So he says there will come a day when God will quench the fires of Hell and set Satan free. He even asks me to hasten the dawn of that day by my prayers and penance."

I chuckled as I added, "And the joke is on me; for he is using my idea of sympathy for God as prod. I'm not kidding. In his latest book Papini asks: 'Has anyone ever realized that this condemnation of Satan also condemns God to suffer at the same time? The punishment of Satan becomes, simultaneously, but in a different form, the punishment of God.' "

"You don't accept any of that, do you, Father? God can't suffer punishment. God won't put out the fires of Hell."

"Not today, Alexie; nor tomorrow. In fact, were He to do so, eternity would cease to be eternity, and God, God. In one of his psalms David tells us that Justice and Mercy kissed. I believe him. That is true. But they still remained Justice and Mercy. But your Papini would have them kiss in such a way that they would cease to be."

I paused there. Alexie waited a moment before asking, "What are you looking so puzzled about? You don't accept any of Papini's thought . . ."

"No, but I'm wondering what happened to his memory. For unless my own is slipping, I believe that back in the second and third century Origen had some such thought about God and Satan.

Yet Papini seems to think his idea is original. It's anything but that. Origen sixteen centuries ago, and then just last century Victor Hugo, came out with the same idea. He not only said the same thing, but claimed he had got it from Moses first, then from Christ. Hugo dabbled in spiritualism, you know. He used a Ouija board, or some such contraption, to make contact with spirits. That's how he met Moses — then Christ. How crazy can seemingly sane humans get, huh? In one of his unpublished poems Hugo has this line: 'Satan is dead; reborn is Lucifer divine!' Of course he has God doing all these wonders; for he ends up with something about: 'All that's base and foul, to love and ecstacy will transformèd be — *by one kiss from God.*' "

"What a line, Father," broke in Alexie.

"Yes, but it's sheer nonsense. And that's more of the devil's work. He has these truly talented men pleading for him. For once the idea of the eternality of Hell dies, Hell ceases to be Hell. Let humans get the idea into their heads that Hell will one day cease to be, and tell me what humans would then go on to be? — Saints? Huh! The devil is clever . . ."

"He's certainly real to you, that's for sure."

I looked at Forrester then and laughed. "Come on down, Alexie, I've got a confession to make." With that I led him to the base of the Tower, pointed to a grassy spot and said, "Sit there and sun yourself while I bare my conscience to you." Once he had seated himself and lighted a cigarette I began, "At my noon-day examination of conscience today I found myself smiling — and all because of you. I was smiling at myself though. For though I hardly ever think of the devil, I have been talking almost incessantly about him ever since you arrived. Yesterday, when I set you listening to the spire, whom did I talk about? — the devil. This morning when I tried to get you to see what was going on in Choir, whom did I talk about? — the devil. Now this afternoon when I bring you up here to meet God, whom am I talking about . . . ?"

"The devil," cut in Forrester.

"Right. Now there is the joke. All I've said about the devil is true. He is loose, I'm convinced of that. Further, I hold we are to blame. We did not listen to God's Mother or God's Vicars. I know that, in very truth, in the sense that Christ proclaimed it: Satan *is* 'lord of this world.' Yet, it is seldom I think of the devil as I've been thinking of him since you came. My Reply to Celestine VI ought to make it clear why. The way I hear *Michael* from my silent spire tells me all about God. The positive side of the First Commandment. I never hear *Quis ut Deus* as a question. I hear it as tribute. No one is like unto God. He is the Great Alone, the Lone Transcendent. Hence, my life and my life's work are one thing — worship. Yet you have brought me to realize, Alexie, that, perhaps for your world and your generation, the negative side of that First Commandment needs to be stressed. Too much idolatry is going on — unrecognized."

"Idolatry — unrecognized."

"You heard me. You heard me yesterday, too. You're going to hear me again later this day. But come now and hurry to Vespers."

With that we started down through the lively spring woods, down the road we had but recently climbed; but during the descent it was I who was as unmindful of the magnificence all about me, for once I had hinted at what I meant by idolatry young Forrester took me up, connected my latest idea with the one that had him so abstracted as we climbed this same road, namely, that our modern world is "possessed by the devil," — and revealed as realities some things I had thought of as only possibilities and probabilities.

As he talked I saw that this young man from far off Africa had been a keen observer of the American scene. Hesitantly at first, but with a nod of encouragement here, and a word of agreement there, I had him soon speaking freely about the immorality and the amorality he had noted among college men and women, the enormous amount of pornographic literature on news stands and book stalls, the over-familiarity allowed among the sexes even in public at football games and in the places of dine and dance after those games. He was frank enough to speak out about the promiscuity he had observed among married as well as unmarried in certain parts of the United States. He used a rather clever play on words when he spoke of the lack, today, of "pragmatic sanctions." With contraceptive devices so easily procured, and with abortion so frequently practiced, he said there was really no "pragmatic sanction" on female or male any more.

I allowed him to talk freely for some time then cut in with the remark that what he was mentioning was as old, almost, as the human race, and not endemic to America nor to his generation. When he argued that it seemed more common over here and appeared to be accepted more casually and even callously, I admitted there might be an increase in recent years, but reminded him that there had been an increase in the human race in recent years. I may have been on the defensive because this young man was a foreigner and was talking about my countrymen and women. But my real reason for objecting to his stress was that I wanted him to see that sex is only one of the devil's tools — and not his most powerful; that the worship of Venus was not the idolatry I feared the most.

He seemed surprised, so I told him that St. John the Beloved had spoken of three concupiscences when he told us "all that is in the world." John spoke of "the lust of the flesh, the lust of the eyes, and the pride of life." He asked what was meant by "the lust of the eyes" and thus gave me opportunity to tell him of the worship given here in America to the one Lloyd Morris called "the bitch goddess" — *Success*. Of course I had to admit that our world was "possessed" by the devil of impurity, but my contention was that the more widespread idolatry — and all but unrecognized by the idolaters — was the worship pragmatic Americans pay to *Success*.

Of course the reality is so cleverly camouflaged by Satan that men, especially young men, can very easily be deceived. The whole affair calls for a clear vision, a keen mind, and a subtle analysis; for every man must succeed to some extent or cease to be a man. Forrester saw this and pressed me for clearer explanation of just what this kind of worship was. I admitted there was difficulty in drawing the line exactly, but insisted the line must be drawn or men would be adoring a goddess, a "bitch goddess," unknown to themselves, committing what has been called "the highest treason: doing the right thing for the wrong reason." It calls for *discretion,* a virtue Dietrich von Hildebrand says has faded from the human scene, and that fading he has named "one of the most serious signs of decay" in our century. Every man must decide just what will be his hierarchy of values — and there is the difficulty. For in our luxurious culture, things of the spirit do not always win first place. To "keep first things first" is our battle; but it is the recognition of what things should be first that shows the difference between idolaters and true worshipers. Money is necessary, I told young Forrester; but it is not the prime nor the ultimate necessity; nor are honor, health, family life, and real human living to be sacrificed for it. Yet many worship at this shrine without knowing they are worshiping. The devil has so deluded them that they think they are doing their duty toward their wives and families when, in all truth, they are actually neglecting their first duty toward wife and family: to give love and share true living — not to sacrifice a whole life just for "the means of living."

Alexie kept me on this "lust" so long that I never reached the one I wanted to reach before we arrived at the Monastery and it was time for Vespers. I left him in the garden between the Gate House and the Monastery with the promise to show him after supper *the* devil who really "possesses" our world, and *the* idolatry that was so universally practiced and universally unrecognized. As I hurried off to Office he sent a typical shaft after me: "Watch universal statements, Father! A single exception destroys their validity!" It was something I had stressed with him early in his visit; for I found him prone, as so many young men are prone, to make universals out of what, at best, are general ideas. Promising I would watch, I went in to Vespers.

After supper I led the boy out beyond the eastern wall of our enclosure where we would be utterly alone. Once I had seated him on a plank that lay across two stumps I took a thin volume from behind my scapular and said, "Alexie, we have been watching the devil at work almost all afternoon. All you told me about sex is his work. I shudder sometimes to see how like pagan Rome we have become — just before pagan Rome fell. The devil of impurity 'possessed' that ancient civilization — and Venus was openly worshiped. We haven't gone that far yet. It might be to our advantage if we did. Open idolatry, I think, is better than worship of a goddess that goes on unadmitted as worship, and even unrecognized as such. I showed you something more subtle when I showed the cult of Success. . . ."

"I'm still having a bit of difficulty discerning the limits of legitimate striving for success, and going overboard and becoming a devotee of the 'bitch goddess.' I like that title. . . ."

"Keep on trying to discern. Pray for *discretio*. But now, this evening, I am going to show you the subtlest work of the devil — and the most dangerous in our day. It has to do with that third 'lust' St. John mentioned: 'the pride of life.' The Greeks had a word for it — *hubris*. Believe me, this is truly Satanic. . . ."

. With that I opened the tiny volume I had brought along, turned to a page well toward the back, and said, "This is Dostoevsky's novel, *The Demons*. Apropos, huh? He wrote it just a hundred years ago. Listen to this passage and see if you do not agree with me that this Russian was truly a prophet." I read:

> The old conception of the world, and above all, the old morality will disappear. Men will unite to extract from life every possible kind of pleasure. The human spirit will be puffed up with pride as great as Satan's, and man will be deified. Ever triumphant over nature, by his knowledge and his will, man will experience by that very fact, a joy that will replace his hopes for happiness in the world to come.

I closed the book and took my seat next to Forrester. "I looked that passage up, Alexie," I said quietly, "just last week. For, recently, I received a report on a convocation of world leaders held in New York City last month. At that convocation a Biologist, who has been a Nobel Prize winner, spoke. The things he said showed me Dostoevsky's man 'puffed up with pride as great as Satan's.' He showed me 'man deified.' "

"Really?"

"Too really, Lex. This man said: 'The Spirit of Science . . .' Get that phrase, for it is pivotal. 'The Spirit of Science, is the spirit of progress. . . . By its means we will ourselves assume the role of creators — and creators of ever lovelier worlds.' That's an exact quote, Alexie. Did Lucifer ever beat that? This man says he and his fellow Scientists are going to become creators. *Quis ut Deus!* Creation belongs to God alone. But this man says he and his fellow Scientists are going to outdo God. Yes, that's what he says; for he claims that 'man is going to create ever lovelier worlds.' " I paused a moment before adding, "When you come to study your Theology you will prove that this is relatively 'the best world.' Yet listen to this man. Now if this Biologist is to be taken literally, has not Dostoevsky been proved a prophet?"

"But, Father, *is* he to be taken literally? Do you really think he actually considers himself a creator? Could he not have been speaking figuratively, using something like poetic license?"

"I sincerely hope that was what he was doing, Lex. But I have my doubts. If I remember aright this man ended with something like this: 'In the forward path of mankind there is room for multifold experimentation and variation, and men can share each other's diverse gains. Thus will the beast in man transcend himself, and the sublime burst forth in a mounting symphony of self-creation.' I more or less memorized that passage because it gives me both hope and despair; despair, because of the blasphemous deification of man I see in it; hope, because of one word. . . ."

When I let the pause lengthen a bit, Forrester prodded me on with, "What word?"

"Beast."

I let the word hang on the air for a while as I looked steadily at my college boy. He waited expectantly. I went on in a lower tone. "Yes, that gives me hope for this Scientist and for his fellows. For if they will be scientific enough to search for the explanation of the presence of the beast in all of us, they and their world are saved."

"Why do you say that?"

The sun had gone down behind the distant knobs but was still throwing pale gold light into the eastern sky. A low-flying robin swooped past with a sharp, commanding whistle. It was the only noise and the only movement in a hushed world. I shifted in my seat and quietly said, "God made each and every man an animal, Alexie. He made none of us beasts. Yet our Scientist is right when he says there is a beast in every one of us. Once he finds the origin of that beast, he will be in the depths of the greatest of all sciences — not Depth Psychology, but what is far deeper: Theology. There he will be face to face not only with man, but with God — if he be sensitive enough he will hear the message of *Michael*. . . ."

"Whoa, Father. Whoa! Not quite so fast. You say there are beasts in all of us. God did not put them there. But when we find who did, we will find God."

"The beasts in us came there from sin. Sin connotes God. It's as simple as that. Immediate illation, if you want to call it such. Or even more simply: correlative ideas. But look what immediately follows: Let these scientists arrive at this discovery, and they will be forced to make the choice every intelligent man is forced to make in life, and for life. Basically, it comes down to heeding Michael's message or rebelling against it. Every man is given but one choice: either to be for God or against Him. Life is as simple as that. Either we will say what Michael said: *'Quis ut Deus,'* or we will echo Lucifer: *'Non serviam.'* Life offers no other alternative. That is why I say our modern world desperately needs to hear our silent spire speak. The need of the day and the hour is for *simplification*."

"You've said something like that before. . . ."

"I'll say it again, again, and again. Of late I've developed a veritable passion for simplification. Your so-called intellectuals force it upon me. For what little I've read of them produced in me what existence has produced in Sartre — *Nausea!* These supposedly learned men have a predilection, it seems to me, to complicate everything. They are past-masters at producing confusion. They fear simplicity. They hate clarity. They abhor definiteness. They are seemingly never at home with anything unless they can claim they find 'difficulties' with it. I had one such intellectual here not so

very long ago who claimed he had 'difficulties' with everything —
even with the principle of contradiction; that self-evident principle,
Lexie, which says 'a thing cannot *be,* and *not be,* at the same time.'
A child of six can understand that principle from what we call 'the
mere inspection of the terms.' Yet this man said he had difficulty
with it."

"You're kidding."

"I wish I were. This man was a University graduate — no simpleton. He told me he had 'difficulties' with the Natural Law, the
existence of God, the multiplication table, every law of logic I
brought up."

"Was he nuts?"

"In my books, of course. But today, and every day, that man
stands before huge classes in a nearby College and lectures the students. He told me I suffer from a fatal defect: I'm too logical."

A roar of laughter was followed by, "What's wrong with
the man?"

"Youth," I said. "Yes, youth. Anyone born before 1930 is not
only out-of-date for him, but out of consideration by him. Youth,
you know, has very little respect today for what we call 'tradition.'
This young man's basic proposition was that he and his generation
— that means you, Alexie! — 'has to re-think everything.' When I
heard that 'howler,' I quietly wished him a very, very long life."

"But you do want us to think, don't you, Father? In fact you
have a habit of making a person think. . . ."

"I want everyone to think *clearly,* Lexie. That's a distinction with
a mighty difference. There is much thought in the world today —
perhaps too much. But there is too little that is *clear* thinking. As I
told you before, that is the devil's work. He is the 'father of confusion.' Then I want *thorough* thinking, or *thinking a thing through.*
There is far too little of that going on — even in the best of circles.
Some of our modern sciences have led fairly good theologians astray
so that, today, almost unconsciously, they have become engrossed
in a study of man rather than a study of God. A French review
brought this out brilliantly a short while back and showed some of
these earnest men that it was not God, as He is in Himself, but

man, the world, and its explanation, that was absorbing them. The review used a sensational title for its examination: *The Atheism of Christians.* Clever, eh? It showed these men that they were making us more and more aware of God as He is *in us,* rather than of God as He is *in Himself.*"

"But where's the atheism if they are making us aware of God?"

"Good question, Alexie. But I will answer it as Cardinal Suhard, the late Archbishop of Paris, answered it. He said this is grafting God on man, instead of grafting man on God. That, you see, is a turning things upside down, a complete reversal of values, and a poison that can be fatal; for that could, ultimately, bring about the destruction of Religion — and a veritable death of God. You see, in this kind of a process, 'the meaning of man' has supplanted 'the meaning of God' — and what has Theology become but some kind of Anthropology? Cardinal Suhard ended his analysis by saying 'Unknown to themselves, many today have become idolaters; they are practicing the idolatry of man.' So you see the idea I sprung on you earlier this afternoon was not original. But you have shown me that Cardinal Suhard's conclusion is sound. Now will you admit the First Commandment is being violated?"

"The First Commandment . . ."

I had to laugh at the bewilderment in the boy's face and voice. "You may have thought I have been rambling around, talking about this and that, bringing in this man and that other rather haphazardly all day, Lex, but I've never wandered from one idea: God — and the worship due Him. I'm still with *Quis ut Deus,* but now I'm on the reverse of the coin — the negative side of the First Commandment — idolatry. You questioned its existence this afternoon, remember? I don't blame you. It is so cleverly carried on and so diabolically camouflaged. But it is real. It is raging. . . ."

"Not as bad as that, is it, Father?" asked Forrester, and there was anxiety in his tone.

I stood up on that, for it was time to start back to the Monastery. "Alexie," I said, "you know much more about Technology than I do. But I wonder if you see, along with the wonders it is producing, the subtle worship it is also bringing on. Here is where I see the greatest amount of *hubris* in actual existence — and in greater potential existence. Let's start back for Compline and I'll outline what I mean. . . ." He arose and we started down the path which borders our orchard.

As we walked along I expressed my admiration for the many marvelous accomplishments already to the credit of Technology. I insisted that God meant man to dominate matter, and, in his own way, but always under God, to rule the world. So it was not with Technology that I was finding fault, but only with some men in the Technological world. Then I told him of the book by Jacques Ellul, a French scholar, which had been translated into English by a member of the Center for the Study of Democratic Institutions, and which had brought to Santa Barbara, in California, thirty of the world's leading thinkers for a Symposium on the problems posed by Technology and presented in Ellul's book. One was: Does Technology relegate Religion to some Limbo? When I told how many of those present agreed that it does, Alexie started. So I regaled him with the joke told at the opening of the Symposium: A future President of the United States is supposed to call in his top experts on computers and command them to construct the biggest and best in the world so that he can ask it mankind's most important question. They do as they are commanded and the President poses the question to the machine: "Is there a God?" Without a moment's hesitation the computer makes reply: "There is *now*."

I was happy to note that Forrester snorted rather than laughed. The story is clever. It is also blasphemous. I then went on to tell my guest how men from many high centers of learning had gathered for this discussion and how some had called computers "omnipotent," others had claimed for them "omniscience," and still others had prophecied that one day soon they would be "omnipresent." It was here I quietly interjected, "Those are attributes of God — and of God alone." I then went on to relate how some at this Symposium had recognized Technology as a Religion, and how one Professor had said that soon computers would be made that would embody all the values and all the virtues men have associated with Athens of old and the Greek philosophers: justice, citizenship, dignity, culture and education, knowledge, wisdom, and the classical trinity of goodness, truth, and beauty. "Never forget, Alexie," I warned here, "that men are producing these machines with all these virtues; men are creating, as it were . . ."

I gave him a few more statements that startle and even strike fear into one who believes in God and knows the First Commandment. But I lightened the frightening report by telling him that one man, a Logician from a University in Jerusalem, had shown what I considered the soundest sense in the whole Symposium, when he stood up and said that he considered computers, and what they could do, "highly over-rated." "Just because they can now write bad poetry and boring music," he snorted, "does not mean that we will one day soon have a robot Bach or a robot Shakespeare."

I resumed with, "But we have robots, Alexie — more and more of them, and man is getting very proud. He will soon think he is *Pantocrator* — Lord of the Universe — Ruler of All. *Hubris* is in the air we breathe these days — and that is another name for Satan. How subtle he is! How clandestinely he works! Now that you've seen something of how he works, you'll be on your guard, I hope."

"But what's the secret of recognizing him?"

"*God-consciousness,* Alexie. The thing I've been talking about ever since you arrived. You and I must become more and more like Leon Bloy. . . ."

"You mentioned him before."

"Yes, he is one of my heroes — as writer and as Christian. He was obsessed, possessed, completely and absolutely dominated by one idea: *God.* Did you ever hear of being 'God-intoxicated'? When you read Bloy you'll understand. But that reminds me . . ."

I then told him Bloy's story of a gypsy woman who, hearing someone speak of the "living God," clasped her child to her breast, swept out of the gypsy caravan and camp, and went about the countryside asking everyone she met to show her the "living God."

"That gypsy woman was and is each of us, Alexie. That's life — and life's whole purpose: to seek and find 'the living God.' Doesn't that simplify matters for you?"

"Yes, if I knew where to look . . ."

I had to chuckle at that and told him about one of Chesterton's poems which has an aged knight who rides "forever seeking God," and who confesses that "though his hair has grown whiter than his thistle plume, and all his limbs are loose, still in his heart one fire burns — a flaming hope that at the next white corner of the road his eyes might rest on Him."

Again I insisted, "That knight is you; that knight is I. That knight is every human being who lives on earth; for by a compulsion deep in our very being, each of us is forced to ride on 'forever seeking God.' Strange as it may seem, that is precisely what the drunken man, the wanton woman, the greedy miser, the prodigal squandering his inheritance on harlots, are doing. They are 'seeking God' — though they are looking in the wrong place!"

The frown that gathered on Forrester's face hurried me into the explanation that these deluded human beings were actually seeking happiness — without knowing that, for the human being, God alone spells genuine happiness. "I know it sounds strange, Alexie, but I also know it is true to say that those who are sinning are actually seeking God in their sinning; for they are seeking joy, though they confuse it with pleasure. God is Joy." I then went further. "These people want love. Of course many of them are taking love's counterfeit — lust; but basically love is what they want, and it was God's beloved who gave us the nature of God in a single word. John said, 'God is *Love.*'"

We walked on in silence after that for a few minutes. But then I resumed with, "Don't think there is anything deep, profound, or original in what I am saying, Lex. It is all very simple. We seek God naturally — by an impulse of our very nature. He made us that way. If you had had more of your formal Philosophy I'd simplify it all still further by saying that each of us is not only an *esse a Deo,* but also an *esse ad Deum.* Which really means that you and I and every human living seek God as naturally as we breathe. The *esse a Deo* and the *esse ad Deum* sounds learned, but it tells you only what any first grader in a Parochial School will tell you when you ask him or her the first two questions in what used to be 'the penny Catechism.' 'Who made you?' and 'Why did God make you?'

The answer to both is the one word *God*. We were made *by* God; and we were made *for* God. You and I; the butcher, the baker, the bandit; the tinker, the technologist, the theologian. Everyone. So you see why I insist on the cry of Michael — *Quis ut Deus*. It is life."

We were near the door of the Monastery by this time so I said, "You asked for an antidote to the sly deceits of the devil and the idolatry to which he leads the unwary. I gave you 'God-consciousness.' I'm going to give you a sure cure for *hubris*. I'll leave it in your room. It will give you a pleasanter night than you had last night, I'm sure. For if you are haunted tonight, it will be by God."

SIX · WITNESSING...THE HUMILITY OF GOD

O N C E Compline was over I hurried to my little office, for the reference I had made to Cardinal Suhard while Alexie and I were out beyond the eastern wall had called to mind something I thought would be the perfect antidote to the *hubris* of man. It was a conference I had given some time back which I had entitled *The Humility of God*.

I found it quickly enough and was just about to rush over to Forrester's room to place it on his desk when the thought struck me that what had been perfectly apt for cloistered monks might not be at all apropos for this college man. I thought it prudent to look the thing over. I sat down and began to read.

"Fathers and Brothers, if this effort lacks finesse and proper polish, blame our good Father Abbot. Of course I have only known of this assignment to give this particular talk for just under a year. But you well know how prudence and practicality always dictate that one never does today what he can put off until tomorrow; and that he is truly a wise man who puts off, until the very last minute, all his really important works. Well, that last minute has been snatched from this truly wise man! Yes, for the old adage came true — even though with an added wrinkle: Man proposes. God disposes. As Dom James forecloses! This talk was originally scheduled for one week from today. Late last night I was told that today was the day it would be delivered. Very well, today it will be delivered. But if its delivery lacks some of my wonted fire — don't blame Dom James. No, blame a lot of medicoes who say I have a 'good heart,' and that it is in its 'right place' — all of which they can prove by X ray pictures; but then go on to say that because that heart is so good, and in its right place, I am liable, at any moment, to 'blow my top.' So what do they do? — They fill me with Snakeroot. Know what that is? — A wonder drug. Yes, indeed; for it makes you wonder just what in the world is wrong with you as it stuffs your sinuses, dries the roof of your mouth, and renders you just about 'half-dead.' I say it is embalming a man's *corpus* before that man is a corpse. However, I'll give you the substance of what I have prepared, with what energy I can summon, and depend on you and your charity to supply the fire — and the fireworks. . . ."

I laid that sheet aside smiling at the literary "conceits" in it; smiling, too, at the memory it revived of the days my doctors treated me for hypertension. I sat in and read more alertly, for, if I should give this thing to Forrester I wanted to be prepared for any comment or criticism he might offer. I saw from the very next sentence that I had plunged into my subject immediately. It read:

"All kidding aside, I am happy, and I know you, too, will rejoice that Divine Providence has so arranged things that, on this Feast of Christ the King, we can spend some time reflecting on Christ's Kingship of Humility as we recall some of the humiliations suffered by this King of kings. . . ."

I had forgotten that it had been on the Feast of Christ the King that I had delivered this conference. That opening sentence practically confirmed me in my determination to give the papers to Alexie; for I immediately felt that no Catholic college boy would lose anything by reflecting on Christ. I continued reading.

"Deus Crucifixus — The humility of God! Was there ever such a combination of words? The humility of God! — Oh, if Moses was on holy ground as he neared the Burning Bush, what shall we say of ourselves who are in the heart of the fire? Yes, the heart of the fire; for we are at the pith of the Passion. Last Recollection

Sunday you heard it was Christ's obedience that saved — and you heard aright. But, Fathers and Brothers, that obedience which saved was but the expression of Christ's humility, as St. Paul expressly tells you in his letter to the Philippians: *humiliavit semetipsum, factus obediens usque ad mortem — mortem autem crucis* — He humbled Himself, becoming obedient . . . Humility expressed in obedience — there you have the character of Christ — and what should be the character of every Christian: humility expressed in obedience.

"But in what mysteries we move! God is a mystery. Humility — is something of a mystery. Join the two and in what a sea of mystery we are engulfed. Yet, as cloistered contemplatives we should know God as few others know Him; and as Cistercians of the Strict Observance humility should be the breath of our life. Do we know God? Do we live humility? — Do we?

"Bishop John Wright of Worcester, Massachusetts, tells what he terms 'the most pathetic story to come out of World War II.' I call it one of the most tragic. It happened on the *Rue de Bac* — that street in Paris where stands the Convent in which the Blessed Mother of God once appeared to Catherine Labouré, and from which we got our Miraculous Medal. A young member of the Resistance Group was skirmishing with some of the Occupation Troops when a bullet from a German rifle ricochetted from the Convent wall, struck the teen-ager, and wounded him fatally. Two nuns rushed out of the Convent and dragged the boy to the comparative shelter of their doorway. Seeing that he was near death, one of the nuns bent over him and said: 'You love the good God with all your heart, don't you?'

"Glazed eyes opened. Then in painful gasps the reply came: 'How can I say that I love Him, this Good God of whom you speak? I have not the slightest idea who He is.' And he fell back — dead.

"Pathetic? — Eternally tragic! Think of it: one gasp from God, one moment from Eternity, one last sentence from his everlasting sentence, and it had to be: 'I have not the slightest idea of who God is.' And the irony of it all: with two nuns of *God* bending over him; — on the *Rue de Bac,* along which so many saints of

God have walked; in the doorway of the Convent where the very Mother of *God* appeared; in Paris, that capitol of a country which for seventeen centuries has rivalled Rome in the things of *God*. That tragedy and that irony highlight our life and our duty: we must make reparation to our humiliated King of Kings. To be ignored is the height of insult — and those who know not God, ignore Him. But the point of all points in this story is that it shows you what is *typical rather than what is exceptional.*

"Douglas Hyde, in his latest book, *One Front Across the World,* tells of three hundred GI's on a Death March in North Korea. With them is a Catholic bishop and a handful of Catholic priests. To fall out of line is to invite a bullet or a bayonet into your vitals. A young GI does fall out. A priest quickly sidles over to him. Seeing the boy cannot possibly go on, the priest says: 'Get ready to die, boy. Tell God you love Him. Tell Him you're sorry for all your sins. Make an Act of Contrition and I'll give you. . . .' A blank face was lifted to the priest. A weary voice all but whispered: 'Padre, I don't know what you're talking about: God — sin — contrition — Got a cigarette on ya?' Think of it: a bayonet thrust away from Judgment and he asks for a cigarette. And again I say: typical, not exceptional. You may cite the psalm and object: 'Father, "only the fool has said in his heart: 'There is no God.' " ' — and I reply: Right! But our world of today is filled with fools! Again that fact highlights our vocation: we must make reparation to our outraged King of Kings; for He is insulted all the day long. His Passion perdures; our love must flame!

"Some of you have seen the book bearing the title *France Pagan.* I believe the English version carries a question mark after the title. I know the original French carried an exclamation point. For it was the devastatingly honest report made by two Catholic priests after their survey of Catholics and Catholicity in and around Paris after World War II. They gave their manuscript to the then Archbishop of Paris, Cardinal Suhard. For three endless days and three endless nights, this always cautious, ever careful, and extremely conservative Cardinal pored over those pages; for he was facing facts he wanted to deny; wrestling with a weight he would throw off — but could not. At the end of the third night of vigil the conservative Cardinal underwent a change and in his place stood a fiery apostle, who came forth with one imperious imperative for priests and laymen alike: 'Go ahead! Go ahead! Never stop! The life of God is at stake. Step forward boldly into a world that is dying for want of you!' — And Paris and the world saw Catholic Action such as has not been seen since Apostolic times.

"Because of that vigil the Cardinal sat down and penned Pastorals that will live as long as men live — for they are masterpieces. One of them, entitled *The Meaning of God,* has much meaning for you and me. The Cardinal gave it that title, for he had found typical what too many were taking as exceptional. He had found that men in Paris, in France, in the whole Western World, had lost the real meaning of God. Irreverance and irreligion were rife because, to most men, God was no longer God.

"The Cardinal points out that too many men treat God as 'Father,' forgetting all the while that He is 'Our Father who *art in Heaven.*' — In other words, forgetting that He is *transcendent.* Bishop Fulton Sheen says much the same thing. He says that men treat God not only as Father, but as some sort of a fairy Godfather. I dare go further and say too many of them treat Him as if He were some sort of a doting Grandfather — forgetting all the time that He is *transcendent.* Perhaps Frank Sheed has struck it off best. He says: 'To millions, God is either an equal or an extra.' That should never be! He is neither! He is *transcendent.*

"I stress that word *transcendent* purposely — and for many reasons. The first is that '*actiones et passiones sunt suppositorum*' — which means that when you have a headache, an eyeache, or an earache, it is not your head, your eye, or your ear that aches; it is YOU who ache in your head, eye, or ear. 'Sufferings belong to the person'; not to the members. I use the word also to make you measure aright. You can never measure depth unless you begin from a height. You will never know the depths of the humility of God unless you begin from the height of His Divinity — and that is really what transcendence means. I use the word that you may know that God *is* God. Finally, I stress the word because the good

Cardinal, in the same Pastoral, speaks directly to you and to me; for he says: 'it is the duty of every cloistered contemplative to remain faithful to his God-given mission; and that mission is *to bear witness to the transcendence of God.'* — Of course! For why have we given up life save to spend it in loving adoration and adoring love of Him who is transcendent — precisely because He *is* transcendent!

"Transcendence — I don't like the word as it stands. I like words that are picture-painting-words. However, if we will stand and stare at this word it may yet paint a very vivid picture for us. If we use a little Reason, some Philosophy, and a bit of Theology we will see. . . . Oh, but I see I am not going to have time to make you stand and stare. . . . So let us turn to the Bible. There we will find what we want to give shape, and color, and texture to this word *trancendence.* Genesis opens with chaos. *Tow-who wah bow-who* is the Hebrew. But then the Dove broods over the Deep. Next, God, your transcendent God, says: *'Fiat lux!'* — and there leaps into being from utter nothingness the blazing sun . . . and it has remained in being and continued its blazing all these billions, and perhaps billions on billions of years. That, simply because your Transcendent God uttered a single word; because your Transcendent God manifested His will. At the same time the moon began to mirror that blazing sun, and rein in the waters for their ebb, and loose them for their flood. And myriads of stars spilled out, each taking its definite place and starting on its definite course — and in that self-same orbit each continued, and some yet continue, and will do so until they burn out after countless thousands of light years. And all because your Transcendent God said: *'Fiat.'*

"As Blaise Pascal said: 'God speaks well of God.' An intelligent reading of the Bible will enable one to see, taste, touch, feel, and even smell, transcendence. It will make that word kaleidoscopic with color, even as it gives it shape as solid and substance as sure and sound as Gibraltar. The wet of rain will remind you of the Deluge and that Transcendent Power who brought it forth. The sight of a rainbow will remind you of the promise of the same Transcendent One never again to use His Power that particular

way. The smell of smoke can be reminiscent of Sodom and Gomorrha — and the insults that forced Transcendent Love to let fall that
brimstone and fire. The sight of the tiniest flame, or the shadow of
a cloud sweeping across the blue, will be for you a *Shekina* — and
speak to you even more emphatically than the Pillar of Fire at night
and the Cloud at day spoke to the Jews of old. For to the Chosen
People then, their *Shekina* told of God's immanence. Your *Shekina*
will tell of God's Transcendence.

"In the Old Testament you will never come face to face with
that abstraction Philosophy calls the *Ens A Se*. That is an absolutely correct description of God. But it will never touch man
where man is most man — in his heart of hearts. You have to hear
God speaking as He did to Abraham; see Him in that Burning
Bush as Moses saw Him; have Him call you in the dead of night as
He called Samuel. The God who appeared to our fathers of old is
not only a personal God but God who is a Person. The God of the
Patriarchs and Prophets, of the Judges and Kings, is anything but
a Metaphysical Abstraction. He is Yahvé, Elohim, Adonai. He is
the Holy One, the Mighty One, the Only One — the Eternal
Alone. He is *Agios O Theos, Agios Ischyros, Agios Athanatos* of
the Lenten Liturgy: the All-holy, All-powerful, Ever-living and
Utterly Undying, Most High God.

"If we once come to know Him as He is, we will be like Jacob
when he awoke from his vision of that ladder which stretched from
earth to Heaven, at whose top was God — and with him we will
exclaim: 'How awesome is this holy place! It is the House of God
and the Gate of Heaven.' We will be like Isaias when he got his
glimpse of God among the Seraphim — and with him we will cry
out: 'Woe is me; for I am a sinful man.' We will be like Ezechiel
when, by the Chobar, he saw the Son of Man amid the blazing
wheels and in the midst of that whirlwind — like him we will fall
on our face; for we will remember: 'It is a terrible thing to fall into
the hands of the Living God.'

"Yes, God does speak well of God — very well indeed. But,
after all our reading, all our study, all our prayerful pondering of
the Bible, from Genesis to Apocalypse, we will end by realizing

more clearly than ever before that God, prodigal though He has been with Self-revelation, remains, and ever will remain, *Deus absconditus* — A Holy God — but a Hidden God — Inaccessible, Incomprehensible, Totally Transcendent! Our only proper response is reverential awe.

"But now realize that this Omnipotent, Omniscient, Omnipresent One; this Being utterly Unique and absolutely Alone; this All-holy, All-perfect, All-beautiful, All-good God; this Totally Other and Universally Transcendent, this one and only Divine Jahvé — became a microscopic bit of protoplasm in the womb of a little Jewish girl who lived in a tiny backwater of Palestine called Nazareth. There is the first — and infinite — humiliation of the Passion of Christ. For the Passion of Christ did not begin, you know, in the Garden of Gethsemani; nor in that Upper Room which saw the Last Supper. Nor, in a certain sense, did it begin even in the womb of Mary. In theological truth it can be said that the Passion began, in a certain sense, before time was; it began back in Eternity, back in the bosom of the Transcendent Trinity. For when God decreed to create a man who would sin, then decreed to save that sinning man by an adequate satisfaction, and the Second Person of the Trinity volunteered to assume human nature to make that satisfaction, the Passion of Christ was on. . . . It will end only when the last man to be saved, is saved. How that first humiliation shows you what humiliation is! It is always something that lowers, lessens, degrades; something that is unbecoming in the sense of unbefitting the dignity of the one humiliated. At the beginning of this talk you saw God is still being humiliated by being ignored. If you will read St. John's Gospel today with this one idea in mind, you will find it one long, loving lament over the fact that God 'came unto His own, and His own received Him not.' It is in the Prologue. It carries through to the very burial. The same is true today. He comes unto His own — and, like Bethlehem before His birth, doors are closed; like Judea after His birth, He must go into exile; like Jerusalem during His Public Life, they will try to trap Him, even attempt to stone Him — Him, the sole Transcendent One! But learn from Him what humility is.

"First, humility is not external. It is of the soul, not of the body! It is in the mind and the will, not in the senses, the feelings, or the emotions. At rock bottom humility is 'a reverent recognition of the Transcendence of God and of our utter dependence upon Him, with the consequent joyous acceptance of anything and everything He sends our way —especially of the untoward which He sends, or allows to come our way.' Grasp this firmly: humility is in the mind and the will, not in the clasped hands, the bowed head, the lowered eyes, the slow gait. It is all inside where man is man, and God is with him. So Bernard was right: Humility is TRUTH. But Aquinas was more right: Humility is JUSTICE. But Benedict and Ignatius were most right: Humility is LOVE! Love! Love! It is based on a vibrantly vital realization of our sonship to God and of His loving Fatherhood which will allow nothing to happen to us that is not, ultimately, for His glory and our own eternal good. It gives peace of mind, happiness to heart, zest for life and living. Above all it bends the soul in constant adoring love and continual loving adoration.

"But time is flying. So let me say that the best thing I have ever read on the subject is in Father Leen's book, *In The Likeness of Christ*. He has a chapter entitled: 'The Humility of Christ.' It is magnificent. But it contains two statements with which I cannot agree. The first is that Christ 'looked upon His humanity, apart from God, as nothing.' Why do I object? Because, Fathers and Brothers, there is no such entity as a thing 'apart from God.' Further, while it is true that God made Christ's humanity 'out of nothing,' it is equally true that He made it into something! The second statement I challenge is the one that states that 'a truly humble man can never be humiliated.' That, I say, is utterly false. For if a man is so hardened that he cannot be hurt, he may be a good Stoic; he most certainly is not a good Christian. Look at Jesus in His Passion and learn that every humiliation hurts. Christ pinpointed and, as it were, protested against the hurt in every humiliation; but then, with supreme self-possession and majesty, He accepted the hurt with humility.

"Have you ever been betrayed by a friend? — It hurts! It hurt

Christ. He protested against the hurt: 'Friend, whereto art thou come?' But then He humbly accepted the betrayal. Have you ever been betrayed by a kiss? — It hurts! Bishop Sheen is fond of saying the kiss of Judas 'blistered the lips of Christ.' But a betraying kiss burns more than the lips; it sears the very soul! Christ pinpointed the heinousness of the hurt with: 'Judas, dost thou betray the Son of Man with a KISS?' But Christ's humility kept Him from turning away His Face. Have you ever been treated as a thief? a robber? — It hurts! It hurt Christ. He protested: 'You have come out with staves and clubs as for a robber. . . .' But in humility, He let them lead Him away. Have you ever been slapped in the face? — It hurts! It hurt Christ. He pinpointed this and protested against the hurt in the house of Caiphas by turning on the underling who had slapped Him and saying: 'If I have spoken evil, give testimony of the evil; but if well, why strikest thou me?' Note the majesty of His calmness. Note the Kingship of His control. The rebuke is there. But He accepts the slap as part of His Father's all-wise plan. That is humility.

"Make the Way of the Cross today. You'll find humiliation at every step — and you'll find that every step was kingly humility! Go through the Passion point by point. You'll find that each was a piercing humiliation. But in each you'll find Christ perfect Master of Himself and of the situation. Why? — How could He do it? — Because He had His mind, will, heart, and whole being ever focused on the truth that God *is* God, the Totally Transcendent — and that He had made Himself sin for us. As you ponder each separate humiliation remember that *'actiones et passiones sunt suppositorum'* — remember that this is the Son of God — true God of true God, who is suffering these indignities; remember He is the Sole Transcendent Divine One who is being humiliated to the depths. . . .

"Have you ever been stripped naked and set standing before a laughing mob? Would you not die of shame were such a thing ever to happen to you? Have you ever once, after you had attained full manhood, been struck with a lash? If so, you know the welt it raised on your flesh was nothing compared to the sting of that lash in your soul! Christ was stripped naked — and in His nakedness set before a laughing mob. Christ was scourged — in the full flower of His manhood! — and scourged to within an inch of His life. But, to me, the crowning humiliation would be to have some human spit in your face. Your whole humanity would revolt. You would be but a primal urge to strangle the one who had dared offer so foul an insult. Look at the Face of God — see all the human spittle that is upon it — *'Passiones sunt Suppositorum'* — This is GOD who is spat upon! What a humiliation — and what humility! He never once turned His Face aside! Can any mortal man again be proud? Can any ever refuse a humiliation no matter how humiliating?

"Fathers and Brothers, it went on to the very end. Even on Golgotha He pinpointed the pain, protested the hurt and the humiliation; but took the injuries and the hideous indignities with true humility. One moment you hear the awe-filling cry of pain: 'My God! My God! Why have You abandoned Me?' The next, you listen to that love-filled: 'Into Thy hands I commend My spirit.' Even after Death they pierced His side to His Heart. Blood and water ran out as if in protest. But that side remained open that you and I might crawl into it, and proceed far down into His very Heart, and there learn the lesson of lessons for life and all proper living: 'Learn of Me — for I am meek and *humble of Heart!*' He Himself would remind us that humility is interior! He Himself would give us the prayer that should be on our lips a hundred and more times a day, and always in our hearts: 'Jesus, meek and humble of Heart, make my proud heart *like unto Thine!*'

"Fathers and Brothers, learn this one truth, and learn it forever: Laurel wreathes *wither*. Rose crowns *fade* and *die*. But crowns made of thorns *endure forever!* If God, in His great kindness, allows you to wear one all the days of your earthly life, thank Him! For He will then, in His great love and wisdom, be allowing you to be very like that Only Son who was, and is, and ever will be King of Kings and Lord of Humility."

I put the last sheet aside. Was this the kind of a talk that would help a twentieth-century college man? For Religious, it was a talk that would be accepted — and, maybe, acted upon. But for those who do not live in Religion . . . I wondered. But then the echo of Cardinal Suhard's cry came to me: "The life of God is at stake!" — That was as true today as it was when His Eminence spoke it. It was as true of Chicago and New York as it was of Paris. It could be true even about South Bend and for some in the great school there. Surely Catholic college men should be involved in what can save the life of their God, I thought. Yes, I would give the talk to Alexie. As I rose from my desk I realized that all I had said about Transcendence in this conference was contained, in a way, in the word I was insisting he hear from our silent spire: *Michael*. That reminded me of some notes I had made when first I had come across that saying by Pascal that "God speaks well of God." I felt these would make the conference even more palatable to Forrester as it gave him a new sense of God's Transcendence, and thus a new height from which to measure the depth of the descent He made when He became Man and then went to death on a Cross. I was especially anxious for my visitor to become acquainted with some of the Canticles in the Bible — and I knew I had transcribed parts from two of those by Moses. I searched for the notes. I finally found them, and on scanning them was surprised to see how much I had forgotten about them. They ran . . . GOD SPEAKS WELL OF GOD . . .

"Genesis speaks well of God as it tells of Creation; Paradise speaks excellently well of God; as does Babel, the Deluge, Sodom and Gomorrha. The Ten Plagues of Egypt speak well of God; as does the Red Sea and the Desert of Suhr.

"God speaks transcendently well of God when He tells of God's Transcendence! God *is* God — there is no other like Him. *Vacate et videte — Ego sum Deus*. Small wonder Moses sang:

Shall I not praise Him — my own God?
Shall I not extol Him — the God of my fathers before me?
Javé — the Warrior God; — Javé — whose very name tells of
    Omnipotence!
How magnificent, Lord, is the strength of Thy right hand;
that right hand which has shattered the enemy —
the hot breath of Thy anger burnt him up like stubble.
What power is there, Lord, that can match Thee?

Who is august in *Holiness* as Thou art?
Who so worthy of *Fear* — and *Praise* —
Who so wonderful in all his doings?

"Better yet is the song this same Moses sang just after he was told he would never enter the Promised Land . . .

Listen you heavens, while I have my say;
Earth, be attentive to the words I utter.
Here is teaching big with import as the rain;
Here are warnings that must soak in like the dew . . .
The renown of the Lord shall be my theme:
To our God belongs majesty;
The God who shelters us, how perfect is all He does;
How right are all His dealings.
God — faithful and unerring;
God — Holy and Just!"

I felt my heart warm again within me as I reread the lines. I was sure Forrester would be as warmed by them. God most certainly had spoken well of God! I put all the papers together and hurried toward the Guest House. It was another night of stars. I was tempted to linger under them; for I can almost hear them singing in such silent, spring nights. But I kept moving. It was only while passing down the corridor of the second floor that I noticed that I had written some lines on the back of the sheet holding the Canticles of Moses. I stopped under the central light and read:

How is it that we can be so careless, so callous? When Moses approached the Burning Bush, off went his shoes; the very ground over which God's Voice sounded was HOLY. When Ezechiel saw the Son of Man in that vision he had by the river Chobar, he fell flat on his face. When Isaias heard the "Sanctus, Sanctus, Sanctus," of the Seraphim, and saw the skirt of God filling the Temple, he cried: "Woe is me! I am a man of unclean lips!" When Jeremias came close to God he was set stuttering. When Daniel was visited by a mere Angel from God, he fell down all atremble. If the creature can be that majestic, what must the Creator be? If the shadow strikes such admiration into being, what will the Substance do? — Yet we of the present day . . . *Do we really know God?*

Try as I would, the reason I had set those lines down would not come back to me. I looked at them a moment longer wondering if they might not negate all I was aiming to achieve by passing these notes on. But then I shrugged. What *do* we know of God? I had insisted He is a Hidden God — but that does not make Him unreal! Far from it. It only makes Him more God — because more mysterious. I placed the papers on Alexie's desk and went to bed.

SEVEN · LEARNING...THE WORTH OF MAN—AND HIS REAL WORK

THE LAST day of Forrester's Paschal visit was one I will not soon forget. It began, as the two previous days had begun, with Mass in the crypt under our Basilica: I, as priest of God, lending my all to the Christ for Him to re-present His Sacrifice; Alexie serving the Mass, representing all Christians — and all mankind for whom Christ had died. It is always quiet in the crypt — a quiet that is truly holy. But that was the only quiet either of us knew that day. For Forrester had hardly finished his breakfast when he began asking questions. I soon saw that he had read both my conference and the note on the back page. Further, it soon became evident that he had reflected not only on those pages, but on every conversation we had had since his arrival — and on the claims of man to knowledge. It was not long before I had plentiful evidence that ideas blow about our college campuses with the same abundance as snowflakes in a New England blizzard.

He began quietly enough, asking about our Cistercian Rite. Then he indulged in some quiet musing aloud rather than engaging me in real conversation; but it was a musing that stirred me much more than it seemed to be stirring him. For after reviewing what he had heard from the silent spire about Michael, Satan, Christ, and the anti-Christ, he softly asked himself (and, of course, me!) how much any human really knew about God. I let him muse on and answer his own question until I caught a note of ever deepening conviction every time he said: "Not much. Not much at all!" I cut in on him there with a Latin quote a professor of mine used on us whenever we needed to be brought up short: *"Putans se putantem."* Still in his reverie, Alexie repeated the quote in a manner I would name "unthinking."

"Right!" I snapped. "Someone 'thinks he's thinking.' That's what that bit of Latin means." Then I plunged. "Alexie, I've heard all you've said before. Many people suddenly think they have made a profound and new discovery when they come up with the query: 'Just what *do* we know about God?' "

"You yourself wrote it. That's what haunted me all night. But I slept. I was exhausted. Yet the first thing that came to mind this morning was your question . . ."

"What question?"

"The one on the back of the conference. . .. "

Then it came to me. I remembered now just why I had contrasted Moses and the Prophets with ourselves. "You mean those lines I wrote about our irreverence?" I asked.

"Irreverence?"

"That's what I was talking about — our irreverence. You did not think I meant our ignorance, did you? We know plenty about God. More, maybe, than Moses, Isaias, Ezechiel . . . What am I saying? Of course we know more than those in the Old Testament! We've had God on earth, garbed in our flesh, walking among men, rubbing shoulders with our humanity and our human way of life, and *revealing*. . . . That's the word: *revealing!* He tore back the veil. He made known. He taught us about God. 'What do we know about God?' Let me reverse your question and ask: What *don't* we know about Him?"

I was aroused by this time; for I had spoken truth when I had told Forrester I had heard this question before. Indeed I had. And these sophisticated agnostics had always stirred me to ire. Their sophistication was so shallow, their agnosticism so baseless. I told this young man now that I had listened to men, supposedly much more learned than he, talk about our meager knowledge of God.

More than one of them had used St. Thomas Aquinas to illustrate their claim. He did say, shortly before his death, that all he had written about God was "so much straw." But these would-be wise men had no idea what Aquinas meant; and surely little knowledge of the nature of his "straw." My indignation was such by this time that I told the boy that I questioned the mental capabilities of these men to lift so much as a handful of Aquinas' "straw," or their intellectual strength to carry a few wisps of it very far.

I see now that I was angrier than I realized, for I recall seizing on that word "straw," and telling the boy that it was this "straw" that had made the bricks which built Universities all over Europe. I can hear myself running off the names: Corduba, Coimbra, Valladolid, Lisbon, Salamanca; Padua, Palma, Palencia and Piacenza; Paris, Upsala, Copenhagen, Cologne; Leipzig, Freiburg, Heidelberg, Vienna. I told him there were at least eighty Universities in Europe before the Reformation — and they all did what Newman said every University should do: point all their courses to the crowning course: *Theology* — the Science of God.

"Do you think those men knew anything about God?" I asked, and then went on to tell how from these massive halls of learning in Spain, Italy, France, Germany, Austria, Scandinavia, Poland, and England, knowledge of God went out and filtered down to the peasants to such an extent that Theology was staple topic for conversation on the streets and in the market-place. I quickly added, "The same thing, or something very similar, has happened in your own day. Thanks to Vatican II, Theology has made the headlines in your dailies, and a subject for article after article in your weekly and monthly magazines — even your slickest. Much of it has been slanted; much of it purely sensational; much even erroneous. But it has been Theology. And I insist again that Theology is the Science of God."

I ended this part of what I now call a "tirade" by giving him some statistics I had happened upon a few days previous to his visit. "The 'straw' that Aquinas talked about, Alexie, forms both the bases and the crowning capitals in our Catholic Educational system here in the United States which happens to total over ten million students in over ten thousand parochial schools, two thousand high schools, and almost three hundred colleges and universities. God is the object studied. Knowledge of Him is the end-aim of this prodigious endeavor. Your Notre Dame would not be, had men no knowledge of God. So don't be deluded. Think clearly. Distinguish sharply. We humans will never *fully* understand God. We have not the capacity to *comprehend* God, if you will take that word in its exact meaning. But that does not mean we cannot *apprehend* Him. There is a mighty difference between knowing all about a person or thing, and knowing nothing about either. God is a Mystery — truly The Mystery of all mysteries. But don't let anyone ever tell you a mystery is something we can know *nothing* about. It is simply something we cannot know *everything* about. You live and move in mystery. But you would be highly insulted if I said you knew nothing at all about them! You can count your heartbeats; but can you fully account for them? You live; but can you tell exactly what life is?"

My outburst shocked him out of his reverie, but sparked him to as animated a discussion as I have ever entered. At some point in my "tirade" I had attacked specialization in Education and said something about while specialists learn "more and more about less and less," it looked to me as if the non-specialists were learning less and less about more and more; and the trouble was that Theology did not dominate and permeate the system. I had also claimed that real Theologians knew much more about the object of their Science — God, than the best specialists know about the object of their particular Sciences. "What does the best Biologist know about life?" I asked. "He stands dumb before a protoplasm. We live in the Atomic Age. What does your greatest nuclear expert really know about the atom? He can split it. He can manipulate it, as it were. But can he tell me just what it *is?* What does your Physicist know about the ultimate constituents of matter? What does your Astro-Physicist or your Astro-Chemist, or your best Astronomer or Astrologer really know about the stars? What does your Psychologist, your Psychiatrist, your learned Sociologist really know about man? I'll put up my ordinary Theologian against the best in any other field and bet he knows more about the proper Object of his Science — God, than they know about the proper object of their specialties. So don't sit there mumbling: 'What do we know about God? — Nothing. Next to nothing.' "

This young man from Rhodesia, an "over-aged college freshman," as he called himself, was not taking that without a demur. He sat up and began to talk.

"Take our medical men, Father," he began, and went on to tell some of the real wonders he had witnessed up in St. Joseph Hospital, South Bend, where he worked after school and on week-ends. I let him go; for this happens to be one of my favorite fields ever since my cancer was excised. I know about the resuscitations effected in surgical suites when a patient has had a cardiac arrest. They are spectacular. They simulate a "calling back from the dead." They are bound to fill any man with a sense of power. But no thinking man will ever consider surgeons as "lords of life and death." Most assuredly, no surgeon will ever consider himself such. He knows his limitations. He is too conscious of the fact that there is no man living who "knows the day or the hour" of his own demise.

I let Forrester talk about the medical world for quite some time; for not only he, with his fluency and his many keen observations, fascinated me, but the medical world itself, with all its wonders, intrigues me. Finally, however, I stopped him with: "Alexie, these men have prolonged life. There is no question about that. Ask any Insurance Agency. But men still die. Obstetrics and Gynocology have advanced beyond all expectations. But we still have still-births, and there is an infant mortality rate! Medical men know much. But the real experts among them who are honest will tell you that what they know is meager, microscopic in comparison to what they don't know. At Mayo's in Minnesota, at Lahey's in Boston, the best of them still have to give as diagnosis 'GOK' more frequently than they care to admit."

"GOK — what is that?"

"The final diagnosis in many a case: *God Only Knows* — what's wrong."

He was more than hesitant about accepting that. It could well be because he is so new to the medical world. However, I did not want to take the tiniest spark from his flaming admiration for the men in this field of marvels, so I led him on to talk about the wonders he had noted in the various Laboratories on Campus. I soon saw that mighty advances and truly astounding changes had been made in Physics and Chemistry since I was in school.

As the boy went on I found it hard to believe that he was only a freshman. Then it came to me how much the curriculum in our colleges has changed. He delighted me with his account. He astounded me with his knowledge. He really tickled me with his enthusiasm. But something in me kept asking: "Are they going too fast? Are they going too far? Are they asking too much? Are they spreading themselves and their students too thin?" It wasn't until I was prompted to ask him how he related all these subjects to the only subject worth a man's total commitment — his final end — that I saw that it was my pedagogical plus my priestly instinct that had had me questioning myself about the prudence — and the profundity — of the system as it is presently in vogue.

"They are giving you much knowledge, Alexie," I said, "but I wonder how much wisdom. Maybe even your educators should listen to my silver spire. He was a wise man who said that 'the soul of education is the education of the soul.' Remember what I told you yesterday about being *from* God and *for* God? God is the beginning and end of Education. Unless you are taught to relate everything to God somehow or other, you are not being educated. That's what I've been saying — at least that is what I have been meaning — when I said Theology is the basis and the crown of education. You've been asking me what we know about God. I am now going to ask you what you know about man. I am really asking your educators what they know about Education. You are not going to college to amass a fund of factual knowledge. It is not information that is the end-object of your education, but formation. Notre Dame will not be truly your *Alma Mater* unless she actually nurtures you to manhood, true manhood, which means, ultimately, Christhood; for He was and is the one model for all men, since He was and is the one perfect man."

He whistled at that. He become excited enough to say I was being narrow; that I sounded as if I wanted to turn modern college campuses into monastic enclosures, and make all young men something like monks.

This outbreak surprised me; for I thought I was but giving, in my own words, the generally accepted idea of Catholic Education. I saw I would have to probe a bit before I went on; for I must come to know just what this young man's idea of a Catholic University was; what the ultimate end of all Education. I thought I could calm him and then lead him on to a revelation of his thought if I accepted his statement and clarified my position as not quite as extreme as he made it out to be. So I told him I knew that the day of the Monastery School had known its nightfall long before he or I had been born. Yet I reminded him that there were those who attributed the making of Europe to the monks who ran those schools, and the making of European cities and present day capitals to those monasteries. I could not refrain, however, from expressing my doubts about the superior efficacy of our curricula, with their multiplicity of courses, over the standard *trivium* and *quadrivium* of those monastic schools of the Middle Ages. "We have more knowledge," I admitted, "but I doubt that we have near as much wisdom." When he remarked that I had offered that distinction and disjunction before and asked me the difference between knowldege and wisdom, I countered by asking him what he considered the marks of an educated man.

He had some very definite ideas about these marks. He spoke readily about culture, refinement, *savoir faire,* polish, taste, knowledge of the arts, and some acquaintances with the sciences. "Truly civilized" was his summation. I congratulated him on his delineation, but then asked him why he was spending so much money going to Notre Dame, when he could acquire all those graces he had mentioned, at a much lower cost to himself, at any State or secular University.

When he came out with the too pat reply, "Because I want to get my Catholic Philosophy," I decided to shock him with the question, "Is there such a thing?" He looked his amazement, so I told him that many a qualified Catholic thinker had asked the same question, and answered it in the negative. "There is, however, and unquestionably, a Catholic Theology, Alexie; and had you told me you had chosen Notre Dame to get all the things you mentioned all colored by and crowned with your Catholic Theology, I would have told you you were making a very fine investment."

"Of course I want that. But Theology is only one of the many courses up there . . ."

"Stop!" I almost shouted. "You missed your orientation in the Orientation Course they should have given you your first days on campus, Lex. Neither Notre Dame nor any other Catholic University or College exists for any other purpose than to so prepare you for life and living that you will attain *God*. In that sense the entire system is Theological; for Education is not education unless it brings one to the Truth, the Goodness, the Beauty who is God. You are not up there to learn how to make a living, you know. You can acquire that technique at a Trade School. You are up there to learn how to make a life, to make a man out of yourself, to learn how to love so that you can attain Him who is Love. You are up there to learn how to integrate your life and living, to unify your whole way of being, to simplify existence by laying unshakable grasp on Him who is Truth. You are receiving a Christian Education so that you may become more and more like Christ. Paul really gave the ultimate for Notre Dame and every Catholic University when he said you are to 'attain to perfect manhood, to the mature proportions of the fullness of Christ.' "

Again he objected, saying I was still too narrow, too insistent on the religious aspect, so much so that I seemed to want to make them all Religious. I was growing a bit desperate by this time, for I knew we would soon have to go to the Conventual Mass. I was not forgetting for the fraction of a second my drive for simplicity, unity, clarity, either; and I, personally, saw the whole matter summed up neatly in the name I claimed came from the silent spire: *Quis ut Deus*. But how get this boy to hear all I heard, and see all I saw?

"See if I can give you my marks of an educated man on the fingers of one hand so that you can have them at your finger-tips," I said. "I say he is an educated man who is truly disciplined in mind, heart, conscience, taste, and social sense. I might put it as he who has a disciplined mind, heart, conscience, taste, and social sense. I will put it that way, for I want you to take discipline in its root meaning and with its full connotation. A disciplined person means a learned, trained, controlled, orderly person. Now he has an orderly mind who can readily distinguish truth from error. He has an orderly heart who loves aright; an orderly conscience who knows the difference between good and evil and does the one and avoids the other. He has an orderly taste who recognizes fair from foul, the beautiful from the ugly. Finally he has an orderly social sense who knows what he owes himself as a man and a person, and what he owes all other humans as individuals made to the image and likeness of God. Sounds like a big order. It *is!* But I sum it up by saying the truly educated man is an upright citizen who is a saint and a scholar. Know any educated men, young man?"

"I'm not too sure now."

"Could it be that you have a warped idea of what makes a saint and a scholar? Could I simplify it all for you by saying an educated man is a lover? He loves the true, the good, the beautiful. But we can't love what we don't know, so we have to know what is true, what is good, what is beautiful. That is why we go to schools like Notre Dame. There you should be developing your ability to think — logically and objectively. Both of those qualifiers are of utmost importance. I like to epitomize all that by saying simply 'think theologically.' You are supposed to be developing your ability to judge; that is, acquiring some discernment, so that you can perceive quickly what is genuine and what is phoney; what is the marrow of any matter and what is merely veneer. You are not up there to get Philosophy so much as a Philosophy of life — and that, of course, is really and radically a Theology for living. The culture you mentioned as a mark will be yours for, if you apply yourself, you will acquire an appreciation of music, painting, sculpture, architecture, the truly fine arts. Further, you'll sharpen your taste and appreciation for good poetry and real literature. We Jesuits always aimed at training the whole man — body and soul, mind, intellect, will, memory, judgment, passions, emotions, imagination — everything — but all directed to one ultimate end — the making of a man on 'the model shown us on the mountain' — Jesus Christ. Herbert Spencer put the Jesuit ideal in other words. He said, 'Education is a preparation for a complete life.' You see how we can take that definition and make it our own, since we know so clearly just what is a complete life: life with God. So now you see how I have capsulized the end of education, the end of life on earth, the end of life eternal in my favorite word: *'God-consciousness.'* "

"But," the boy objected slowly, "if all you say is true, there is no real education outside Catholic Colleges. . . . You wouldn't dare say that would you, Father?"

"I might dare say more. There is much learning outside Catholic Colleges, very much. I dare say much more than there is in Catholic Colleges. But the fact remains there's very little real education without Religion. Your answer depends upon how much Religion there is on campuses other than Catholic. I know it sounds narrow to you. But actually it is the least narrow of any of the concepts of Education. Alexie, you've shown me that you — and maybe all like you — need to be made rightly *self-conscious*. I've insisted much on God-consciousness, haven't I? Well, now I'm going to be just as insistent on man-consciousness. For that may lead you, and others through you, to correct God-consciousness. Do you know what a man is?"

Before he could answer, the bell rang for the Conventual Mass. "Come," I said, "and you'll see man at his natural best. Get that word 'natural.' It is pivotal. Next, you'll see man at his noblest, performing the most magnificent act any human being is capable of performing. You are going to see man standing at his tallest, expressing his personality with rare perfection and true fullness. You will see man in the most personal, intimate, humble, yet most exalted relationship with God possible this side of the Beatific Vision. You will witness man doing precisely what he was created to do. This will be true Education if you will be both God-conscious and man-conscious."

With my hand on the doorknob I paused for one last directive. "You are going to see what Nietzsche never saw: real Supermen — or Overmen. You will see what Satan mimics again and again. If you will but open your eyes, you will see God — and you will see yourself as you really are — as you look into the eyes of Him who made you. . . . I'll see you in the garden after Mass."

I went down to my place in choir still somewhat warm in body as well as mind because of the morning's interview. But once we moved into the Mystery of Mass I quieted and saw that I was not wrong in stressing the fact that in this Act man is at his best. I believe it was at this point that I resolved to make Forrester keenly *self-conscious* by making him truly man-conscious.

We met after Mass and I wasted no time in getting to my point. "Well, did you see how natural it is for man to do what we just did at Mass?"

"Natural? I thought that was the most supernatural thing a man could do . . ."

"It is. But I was using the word natural as meaning according to nature. Man is a worshiper by nature, Alexie. Man must adore if he will be true to himself. And I would hazard the statement that Education's aim is to show you whom to adore. Worship is as natural to man as breathing."

That started my guest telling about Africa and the tribesmen there whom most of us would call "savages." No formal education whatsoever was theirs; tribal customs governed their entire way of life; and there was much voodoo. Forrester held me in wrapt attention as he recounted experience after experience among the natives of his land. Some were enough to chill the blood — as he told how he had to witness the murder of newly-born twins simply because witch-doctors claimed they were an evil sign on the parents and the tribe. Others were scalp-tingling — as his account of how some stupid-seeming fetish led to savage slashings of one's self which approximated, when they did not result in real, suicide. He told me of the power witch-doctors held — and used — over the people. He described charms, amulets, talismen. He ended with, "I'd call much of it ignorance, most of it stupidity, some of it truly diabolical; but what can I call religious? What real sacrifice or worship? Black Magic is what most call it."

"Most whites," I corrected. Then I showed — or tried to show — that many of the practices he had told about were founded very definitely on man's instinct for worship. These poor people know, as every thinking man knows, that man is dependent; that there is Someone over him; that that Someone should be worshiped. I pointed out what, to some extent, were parallel practices among our North American Indians, as witnessed by the early Jesuits. I told how classmates, now in India, had written, telling me how aborigines over there, with no culture save their own primitive culture, sacrificed to a Supreme Being. I then concluded that it was natural for man to worship and insisted that any man who did not pay some sort of homage to a Supreme Being was unnatural, hence, no real man.

"See why I say it is as natural for man to worship as it is to breathe. That's a trifle hyperbolic, of course, since we have to breathe more frequently than we need to actually worship. But you get the idea. These savages of yours, and these primitives of mine, have clearer ideas on what it is to be a man than many of your so-called educated. I know I'll shock you, and I'm sure I'd shock many of your Professors, when I say the ultimate aim of your College Education is to make you *properly self-conscious;* to give you the true concept of what it is *to be a man.* To simplify it all for you I point to that silent spire up there and say *Michael. . . .*"

"Hold on, Father. You give me one word from that spire, but you make that one word say many, many things. First it was God; then it was Satan; now you want it to speak of man. . . ."

"I've had it saying one thing only, Lex: *Quis ut Deus.* That connotes the First Commandment. That Commandment tells you as much about man as it does about God, if your ears are attuned."

"Mine aren't attuned, then. I like the idea of that spire saying *Michael.* I'm glad to know the meaning of that word: *Who is like unto God.* I'll even take that to mean the *First Commandment.*

But how in heaven's name you get man out of that Command which tells all about God . . . 'I am the Lord, thy God. . . .' "

"Stop there, Mr. Forrester!" I said laughing. "You've said it all."

"I said it all? 'I am the Lord, thy God . . .' says it all?"

"Don't be so indignant. Don't be so incredulous. Think! 'I am the Lord, *thy*. . . .' To whom does that pronoun refer? To *man!* And it is telling you what man is as you'll never learn from the kind of Philosophy they are giving you if it is that thing you described for me yesterday — a mere History of Philosophy."

"Come on, Father. You're getting cryptic; and what is cryptic is anything but clear — at least to this man from the African bush."

"Alexie, that pronoun in the First part of the First Commandment is the most precious word in all literature as far as you and I and our fellow humans are concerned. I'll go further and say it is the most precious word, the most indicative in any Philosophy, Science, Art, Literature, or Theology. It indicates what you and I *are*. God is saying that you and I are *His!* That we belong to Him. That we are His relatives. That we bespeak a relation to Him. Have you ever heard man defined as 'a relation to God' or as 'God's relative'? Those are apt definitions; much more exact than the one with which you, most likely, are much more familiar; namely, 'man is a composite of body and soul.' That is a false definition if you want to know; for it is an incomplete definition. You and I are more than 'composites of body and soul'. . . ."

"What are we then?"

"Composites of body and soul *and God*."

"Whew!"

"Whistle all you want. You are but manifesting the thing I've been combatting for years — failure to think a thing *through*. I don't blame you, Alex. It's almost universal today. But from now on I want you to be more thorough. You know I like to use the word 'dialogue' in its root meaning from the Greek '*dia-*' meaning *through;* '-logue' is from *logos* which can mean to 'speak,' but I like to press it to its fullest extent and say it means to 'speak logically.' Hence, to me 'dialogue' means talking a thing through and through, logically. Let's do it with the idea of man. You say, usually, he 'is a creature composed of body and soul.' That's an exact definition. But note that I have put the word 'creature' where we had 'composite' before. See the mighty difference? I wonder just how you would define creation for me. Have you had that in your Philosophy as yet — or your Theology?"

I saw the hesitancy in Forrester's whole mien, so I went on: "Most people define creation as 'the production of something from nothing.' That is not true. That is not creation. Such a definition will never tell you or me whence we came."

"We came from nothingness, didn't we? — I always thought so."

"I hope they do not drop Scholasticism, Lex. If they don't you'll learn the axiom that — 'From nothing, nothing can come.' Obvious, isn't it? Yet, look at what you just said: You've always believed that we came from nothingness. See what I'm driving at? I'm trying to make you properly self-conscious, truly man-conscious. I'm trying to make you see that to be a creature is a dignity beyond compare; to be a human creature is to know an exaltation that is literally measureless; for it tells of our relation to Infinity, to Transcendence, to Eternal Life, Love, Joy, Being — to God!" I paused long enough to prepare Forrester for my climax. "Creation, my boy, is 'the production of something from nothing . . . *by the action of God'!*"

"I always knew that, Father. Maybe I did not always express it that way. . . ."

"But that's the whole point, Lex. To be properly *self-conscious* is to be truly *God-conscious;* for you are not only a 'relative of God' you are a *'relation to* God.' Oh, if you only had your Scholastic Philosophy on Relations, what a thrill you would know every time you became properly self-conscious. . . ."

"I've studied something about Relations. . . ."

"Good! Then you know that there must be two terms before there can be a relation. I often think of electricity when I think of this doctrine. I can't have a current unless I have two poles, can I? One must be positive, the other negative. Look on God as the Positive. Look on yourself as the negative, and realize that life is a current flowing from Him to you and back to Him again. That's what man is, and that's what life is: a relationship to God! Grasp this truth, Alexie, and you'll ever walk with head high, shoulders back, and step firm; for you are a work of Omnipotence, and one He, the only Omnipotent, must keep on working. You've heard the Irish say: 'God hold you in the hollow of His hands.' He does. Always. Else you'd drop back into the nothingness from which He called you into being. To be a creature is to be dependent on and from God every moment of your creaturehood — or your existence. But what a dignity that is! And there, precisely, is the indignity I see done to man by those idolaters of man."

The boy's eyes were question marks. I chuckled. "Alexie, I'm not going to move from the First Commandment all day — so don't look surprised when I harp on idolatory and insist upon adoration. Many of your big-hearted Humanitarians are actual idolaters. They serve man for man's sake — and for man's sake alone, without any reference to God. That is to insult man as well as insult God. You've heard God saying to Moses 'I am the Lord, thy God; thou shalt not have strange gods before Me. . . .' You must have heard Christ say to Satan: 'The Lord, thy God, shalt thou worship, and Him alone shalt thou serve.' That gives you clearer understanding of my claim that Education's ultimate aim is to teach you how to avoid idolatry and show you whom to adore; whom to serve. If your service to man is not service to God, Alexie, it is what the Jews of old would call 'fornication' — what I call 'false worship' or 'idolatry.' "

"Hmmm. Not many of us think that way, Father. But I must admit it is the proper way to think. God-consciousness is the key, eh?"

"I'm drilling on man-consciousness today, Alexie. I'm laboring to show you what real *self*-consciousness will do to a man. It will make him a saint. . . ."

"Whew!"

"Well, I suppose I can't blame you for whistling again. But you do test my mettle. O.K. But let me take up one other whistle of yours first. You thought I was more than hard on non-Catholic Education earlier this morning. Actually I was being as hard on some Catholic Educators, Lex. The whole thing centers on the true concept of Education; which, in turn, rests entirely on the true concept of man. We don't educate horses, cows, or dogs, you know. It is only man. Animals are to be trained. The rational animal is to be educated. Not to be instructed; not to be informed; but educated. Ultimately, Education is not so much a matter of putting in, as it is of bringing out — and, of course, you know what I'm driving at: True Education will bring out the image and likeness of God that is in man, and the character of Christ that is stamped on every person baptized. Just as man is always saying a relationship to God, so all Education should be saying the same thing; for it is always dealing with God's relative — man. How, then, can there be anything like real Education where there is no orientation or even any reference to God . . . ?

"But, Father, there is such a thing as 'Secular Education . . .' "

"There is a thing called that; but it is 'secular'; it is not 'education.' Frank Sheed did a brilliant job on this contention of mine once. He found the State just about monopolizing Education in the Western World. So he spoke to the State, and said: 'I see you're in the business of "fitting man for living" — that is the generally accepted definition of this business of Education in which you are engaged. Now can you tell me what a man is?' . . ."

I saw the boy's attention quicken. I smiled. "Do you think the State would give any of the definitions you and I have given this morning? Yet, what other definition is there that will hold water? Man is a creature. . . . If we stop there we have all we need to show all Education must be God-oriented. For creature bespeaks continued dependence on the Creator. The illustration I like best is that taken from our own definition of a man. We say he 'is a creature made to the image and likeness of God.' That is man's being — an image. How long does an image stay in a mirror? Only so long as the object reflected therein stands in relation to the mirror. Since you are an image of God — always were and always will be — don't you see how near God is to you — and how 'like unto God' you must always be? How to be that way is what Education is supposed to show you. That's what Education is all about ultimately. So you see where Frank Sheed was driving. After showing the State had no acceptable answer to his question about man, he went further and asked the State about 'living' — for we all agree that Education is to show one how to live. But, Alexie, I can't show you how to live unless I know what life is all about; what living is for. I must know the purpose of your existence. . . ."

When I paused the boy broke in with "To get to Heaven, ultimately."

I laughed at that for he gave me an opening I was not looking for. To his quizzical glance because of my laughter I said, "Only saints get to Heaven — and a second ago I heard somebody snort at the idea of becoming a saint. But, tell me, do you know of any state in this Union of ours that would answer Frank Sheed as you have answered me? We'd have a Supreme Court case on our hands immediately. If any state said the purpose of its State University was to help its citizens so to live that they might attain God — might get to Heaven — there'd be an uproar! The First Amendment would be called upon. There'd be headlines in every paper; articles in every magazine; protests would be organized. Yet, what is Education for? See now why Frank Sheed, in his cool, clear English way said: 'This situation — of the State being *the* Educator — is taken as normal, whereas in fact it is grotesque.' Later he stated: 'To call it grotesque is to flatter it. For to be fitting men for living without knowing either what man is or what life is all about — is odd beyond all words.' "

"Gosh! Father. Who'd ever think of that?"

"Frank Sheed did. I do. I want you to. But the fact that so few have done so, Alexie, shows the need for what I referred to as real dialogue — the need to think a thing through — and think it through logically. Not many people would get excited about such a situation; for there are not many people who think deeply, think about fundamentals; think about ultimates. I'm trying to make a 'Fundamentalist' out of you, Forrester. I'll succeed if I make you properly *self-conscious*. That spire can do the job for me, if you will hear the word *Michael* aright. I'm back to the First Commandment again. I promised you I'd never leave it."

I then said, "You were made for one ultimate purpose, Alexie. Not to 'get to Heaven' as you said a moment ago, but to do on earth and in time what you are going to do in Heaven for all Eternity — if you get there. *You were made to give God glory.* That is the only explanation of your sitting here this moment under this Japanese lilac tree." With that I began with the Triune God and showed the boy that God cannot act except for His own glory. Were He to do so, He would cease to be God. Hence, all creation, animate and inanimate, rational and irrational, human and angelic has but one purpose: to give glory to God. I showed him that the sun gave God glory by being itself — by being the sun; that a glow-worm did the same thing in the same way — by being a glow-worm; and that man could give it only by being a man — which means an image of God. I paused here and said, "But there's the rub. Man *is* an image of God. Therefore, he is free. Hence, the glory he gives to God should be in accord with his nature — free. Man should glorify God deliberately, of free choice, with set determination. But . . ."

Here a truth struck me that I thought might help emphasize my point. "Strange as it may seem, at first, Alexie," I said, "even the atheist, the agnostic, the profligate, the wastrel, and the scoundrel will give glory to God ultimately — and give it to Him for all Eternity. But it will not be the formal glory planned by God to be given by His human creatures. It will not be freely given. It will be extracted, as it were by the Justice of God. Satan is giving glory to God right now just as well as Michael — but with what a difference! Michael gives it freely — out of love. Satan gives it against his will; or better, God's Justice extracts it from him from Hell. So you see God is going to get His glory — for he is a jealous God."

I saw the boy's head jerk at the word "jealous." I smiled and said, "Yes our God is a jealous God, Alexie. He told us so Himself. Prodigal though He is with His love, goodness, truth, and beauty — which we see lavishly flung out all over the universe — He is very jealous of His glory. That is what Isaias tells us: 'Thus saith the Lord God who created the heavens and stretched them out; who established the earth and all things that spring therefrom; who giveth breath to the people who tread that earth, and spirit to them that walk thereon . . . *I, the Lord, that is my name — and I will not give my glory to another.'* I love that passage. I memorized it years ago when Ignatius took me into what is called the Long Retreat and taught me truth through his Fundamental Exercise. That 'exercise' really comes down to this one thought and truth: Man was made to give glory to God. 'I, the Lord, that is my name — and I will not give my glory to another.' That is why the Jesuits have *A.M.D.G.* as their motto 'To the Greater Glory of God' — and why we Cistercians have *U.I.O.G.D. —* 'That in all things God may be glorified.' See how easy the transition from the Jesuits to the Trappists was for me? They both want their subjects to live ever properly *self-conscious*. Need I say again that that means truly *God-conscious?"*

"Hardly," he answered and there was that in his voice which told me I had reached saturation point with that phraseology. We sat in silence for a short while after that, but when I caught his eyes on the silent spire I quietly said, "Now you must see why I love the Trappist way of life, Lexie. You'll hear people use the expression about 'burying themselves in a monastery.' You'll be in position to show them that here we really come to life; for our every hour of day and night is spent fulfilling the one purpose God put man on earth to accomplish — and in so doing truly fulfill ourselves. People are often puzzled to note how happy Trappists appear. Those people are like the State Frank Sheed talked to — they don't know what man is, or what life is for. If they realized, Alexie, that you — and every other human — are basically nothing but a hunger for the Absolute, a thirst for the Infinite, a passionless passion for the Eternal, simply because you are a man — then they would understand the atmosphere of Gethsemani and the aura each monk carries about him. It is not an aura of happiness so much as of joy. For these monks are men who go always groping after infinite things, just because they have already laid hold on them; men who go ceaselessly searching for the Simple, the Sublime, the Beautiful, just because they have already found Him who is Simplicity, Sublimity, faultless, flawless, Infinite Beauty. That is why they can

be summed up in the one word: *Adorers.* They have to be that because God is God and man is man, and these monks are truly self-
and God-conscious. They realize that they are both relatives of God
and relations to Him. They adore — and their adoration is all *love."*

When Alexie simply nodded in acceptance I decided to stir him
by going back to my claim about the purpose of his higher education. "When you graduate from that famed institution up there in
South Bend — too famed for football, maybe" I said, "if you are
not a lover, your four years will have been wasted." He looked at
me with rekindled interest and rekindled puzzlement. "That's all
any Catholic College or University is supposed to turn out, Alexie
— lovers." He smiled at that, as much as to ask: "Now what are
you up to?" I returned the smile and said, "The most common
expression for a passionate lover to use toward his beloved is: 'I
adore you.' See what Trappists are? Passionate lovers. See what
you must become — not a Trappist — but like a Trappist: a passionate lover of God and men. That's what a Christian is — and I
hope Notre Dame graduates Christians still. Adoration is love, or
it is not adoration. And love is adoring — literally, when applied
to God — metaphorically, when applied to our love for humans,
or it is not love. So you see what's wrong with the world: Not
enough adoration — too much idolatry. And I blame your Nietzsche for that. He has led man to the worship of man. The steps
are logical: if God be dead, and if it be man who has killed him,
man is greater than God . . . is already Superman. Look at the
results: Shake off the 'tyranny' of Religion; get rid of the 'opiate'
of the people; blot out that 'one immortal blemish of mankind'; and
people will become aware of their sovereignty, know their absolute
independence, revel in their complete freedom. The human race is
logical. But just look at the 'joy' Nietzsche's directive has produced:
Wars, and rumors of more wars. Famines despite the earth's fertility. Murderous racial strife despite declarations of fraternity and
equality. Discord almost universal despite the United Nations. In-
evitable, I declare it. Perfectly logical. Displace God, and everything
goes! Anything at all is permissible to the Superman. But when
there is more than one Superman on the earth, how can there be

peace? Logical it is. Without God there can be no love."

Again a silence fell between us. I finally broke it by rising from the bench and asking, "Do you see why I want the world to hear the silent spire? why I want Michael's message thundered to modern man? — For man's sake, Alexie, as well as for God's. Think what a world we would have if every man were properly self-conscious, if he knew himself to be a relative and relation to God, if he realized his one purpose was to love. Dream of what it would be like to live with lovers who were saints. You snorted at the notion of you becoming a saint, didn't you? I've already blasted your delusion, I hope, by reminding you that Heaven is your home, your destination, but that no one gets into Heaven but saints. Now let me tell you it is not as difficult as you imagine. Satan is in your delusion. Discouragement is his most useful, and most used, tool. Let me be brief — for dinner is almost upon us. I'll take Lacordaire's definition and simplify, clarify, and unify all for you. He once said: *'Duty done spells sanctity.'* Do your duty, and you'll arrive. I put it more pithily. I say: *Be yourself — and you'll be a saint.* By now you know what I mean by being yourself — You are a son of God. 'Like Father, like son.' He is Holiness. Can you be yourself unless you are holy? After dinner I'll make you more self-conscious and show you the 'more excellent way' as Archbishop Goodier of Bombay once called it."

EIGHT · LOVING...GOD—SELF—AND MAN ARIGHT

I **DID** not get to that "more excellent way" immediately; for when I joined Forrester under the shady ginkgo he was a veritable fountain of questions. He had heard the rumble of heavy guns, learned they were being fired at Fort Knox, some twenty miles away, and quite understandably wanted to know what I thought about America's part in the Viet Nam trouble. That led, of course, to queries about my opinion on the probability of a Third World War. Soon he was asking me about the Peace Priests, Religious taking part in Civil Rights Demonstrations, draft-card burners, and the individual human holocausts for the sake of outlawing war.

It was a difficult half-hour for me; for I find all these matters delicate. Further, my convictions are so deep and set and my temperament such, that I can wax passionate on just about every one of these topics. But I had to remember I was a priest talking to a lay person; I was a cloistered contemplative monk talking to a college freshman; I was an American — and an ardent American — talking to a non-American.

He manifestly was much better informed than I on the world situation, and actually surprised me with his knowledge of international politics and policies. I, of course, could only enunciate principles and make the best possible and practical application to the general ideas of war, peace, civil rights, individual duties, and personal responsibilities. But I did have something which held Forrester's attention. I believe it was my adherence to principle and my insistence on logic. Even with those two in my favor, I still found myself growing emotional on some of these matters, and I grew fearful that my feelings might well up too far. The guns kept rumbling and Forrester kept asking about war. It wasn't until he had made a remark which I took to be a slur on our American troops in World War II that I lost my control to some extent. "Let me tell you something," I snapped. "These Coca-Cola drinkers and Camel smokers that you tell about; these American GI's who lived so luxuriously as you claim, are the boys — and I use that word advisedly — for they *were* mere boys — are the boys who saved Europe in 1918 and the world in 1945. America never had compulsory military service until lately, you know. Yet, back in 1916 and '17 we took kids off the campus — yes, kids like the ones you are sitting with in class these days — put them in uniform, gave them a gun, a few hours, comparatively speaking, of training, then shipped them to France to whip the greatest military machine ever got together since the days of Napoleon. In eighteen months they did what France, England, Italy, and the rest could not do in over two and a half years. Then, after being attacked when unprepared in the early 1940's, we once again girded our loins and battled not only in Europe, but in Asia and Africa, in the Atlantic, the Pacific, and the Mediterranean and smashed that outfit, which had blitzkrieged every country on the continent, and the mighty army, navy, and air force of a militant Japan. The kids may have wanted their Cokes as you say — and their Camels, but they were able to do with those what all Europe and all Asia were unable to do. I'm proud of the American Doughboy and the young American GI — and while I have respect for every country and every man who ever shouldered a gun, I'll never allow anyone to say the kids from our campuses did not show mankind what it is to be an American, what it is to have mind, will, imagination, ingenuity, and just plain guts."

Judging from the look in Forrester's eyes, I realized that the warmth with which I spoke must have surprised him. "Remember, Alexie," I said, "Patriotism, or love for one's country, is a very Catholic, Christlike virtue. Next, remember virtue and virile and the word that means man — *vir* — all have the same root. I'm a man. I couldn't be a monk unless I was a man. I'm an American Catholic. I love America and Americans. I'm proud — proud as the proverbial peacock — over what our American kids did in the two World Wars. And what I said before about saving Europe in 1918 and the world in 1945 is history not hyperbole."

"Sorry, Father. I did not mean to cast any aspersions on the American fighting man. I did hear that they would not move unless they had their Cokes and their Camels. It may have been idle gossip . . ."

"It may also have been jealousy that is anything but idle . . ."

"I suppose it could be. I guess what I was looking for was some argument for peace. Or maybe just a clarification of my own ideas about some of the boys up in South Bend. We've had our excitements at Notre Dame, you know. Nothing like Berkeley, of course, but enough to make one think. Some of these 'peaceniks' are powerful talkers. Some have arguments that I can't answer — and yet arguments I don't like to accept. I feel as deeply as you, Father. I'm part Irish, you know."

I laughed at that, and the tension was broken. I asked him, then, for some of the arguments he found unanswerable yet unpalatable. He had them very clearly. I had heard some of them before, and read others in Theological Reviews. I let him talk himself out. He gave the arguments and his efforts at refuting them. I found both very interesting. But when he came down to saying that it looked to him that nowadays no Catholic could possibly defend war I stepped in.

"Not even John the XXIII with his *Pacem in Terris* held that, Alexie. Think with the Church and you'll be safe. Paul VI never gave out such a statement as the one you've just made. Even Vatican II admits there is a 'just war.' Oh, I know your bright avant gardists have laughed at such Moral Theology. But let me tell you those bright young boys don't know Catholic Moral Theology. What they are laughing at never was taught in the schools, and was never held by any intelligent priest. Chesterton gave it all magnificently when he said: 'The only defensible war is a war of defense.' The Popes have said the same thing in different words — and they will continue to do so until 'skies be fugitives. . . .' "

" 'Skies be fugitives,' " he echoed. "What in the world does that mean?"

"So long as man is man. We have not only a right, but a duty, an obligation to preserve our lives — and to ward off any and every unjust aggressor. What is true of the individual man is true of the moral person called the State or Nation. That principle is unassailable, and will be applicable so long as men are born of women, for it is eternally true. Of course I'm all for peace, for arbitration, for negotiations, for 'reasoning together,' as our President would say. I'm very far from 'trigger-happy,' Lexie. But I'm not too sanguine about man and his control of his selfishness. I fear his acquisition of power. Have you realized that the more mastery man attains of matter, the more physical power he acquires, the less moral stamina he manifests? Morals are falling. There is no doubt about that. We can't be ostriches. But how many have noted that there is an evident proportion to their falling and the rising of Technology? Romano Guardini has a very provocative thought on this matter. He says that the very power which man has taken into his possession — without any reference to God — will be the very instrument God will allow man to use for his own punishment."

"The bomb, huh? Does Guardini think it spells genocide — the end of the world?"

"I'm not too sure of that, Lexie. It could be Guardini's thought. But if it is, I want you to note how free he is from anything smacking of Manichaeism. He is not saying that matter will destroy the material world, but man — and man doing it *only* with the permission of God. I say that because I suspect that many today are becoming unwittingly Manichaean as they think on and talk about Technology. Remember what I said yesterday about those 'mechanical brains. . . .' They are not human; they have been made by humans.

They are far from being gods — though some people all but adore them. This world will be destroyed in God's own time and in God's own manner; not a moment before, nor in any manner other than the one He wants. God is God. This world is His world. And man, with all his power, is but a puny little creature compared to the Creator Omnipotent. God does have an infinite respect for the freedom He has granted us humans, and it may be that He will allow us to use it foolishly. But if He does, it will be under His domination and with His permission — not at man's defiant election. The bomb, with all its potency, has never scared me. Nor does man with all his madness. For I know God is God. Above all the turbulent waters of the world I see Christ walking, and I hear Him saying what He said that night on Genesareth's Lake: 'Fear not. It is I.' How can any believer ever be afraid?"

"Oh, Father! Aren't we all afraid?"

I laughed at that. "See any fear on the faces of these monks?" He did not answer my question nor my laugh. "I suppose I sound naïve, Alexie, to any who come from your very sophisticated world. But never forget what my naïveté is based upon — *Faith*. I believe. That gives the simplicity, clarity, and unity to my life I've been talking about since you arrived. Don't think a simple man is a simpleton. I know Science has given man more power than man ever had before. I know power intoxicates. I know drunken men are dangerous. How could anyone who has lived in this twentieth century fail to know all that, with the Kaiser, Hitler, Stalin, and a host of others to remember? I even know how drunk some men are today. What Gothic Cathedrals were for the men of the Middle Ages, launching pads down on Cape Kennedy are for many a man today. Actually, they are places of worship. Atomic reactors, for some, are veritable shrines. Just last week I heard from a man whom I had on my Debating Teams up at Holy Cross back in the 1930's. He had just been down into that War Room — or whatever they call it — out there in Nebraska. You know the place I mean: the Room with the radar screen that can show, so I'm told, every ship in the air, every submarine in the waters of the world. My friend was taken down into the heart of this magic, this monstrous thing. He had been here just a week previous to his visit to Nebraska. He wrote me many things about that Room, but the thing that stands out is this: he wrote 'This place is Gethsemani upside down.' Since he looks upon Gethsemani as the vestibule to Heaven, you can see what he thinks that War Room is the vestibule to. Sherman did say something about war being anything but Heavenly, didn't he?"

"Who's Sherman?"

I had to chuckle at that. " 'Scuse me, my boy. Every now and then I forget you are not an American. Sherman was one of our outstanding Generals in our awful Civil War. He said: 'War is Hell.' No one will argue with him on that, will they? But why not face facts: we are at war right now. Have been since the end of World War II. We could call it something of a 'cold war' once, but not today with Viet Nam escalating and escalating, and hot spots here, there, and everywhere around the globe. Yet it takes no great student of History to see what is going on. I told you yesterday. The Two Standards are clearly discernible. The Two Leaders are unmistakably recognizable. The Two Armies, no matter what diplomats, heads of States, politicians and journalists say, are very definitely drawn up. St. Ignatius was right: God and Satan are fighting — not for global territories, but for the souls of men. That's the only war to be greatly concerned about. That's why I want the world to hear what Fulton Sheen called 'The Thunder of Trappist Silence' — and I call the word from the silent spire. How the men of this day need to hear: 'Fear not! It is I! . . . It is I . . . Yahwe. . . .' "

It must have been this last that plunged me into some sort of a reverie in which I repeated the Names of God as found in the Old Testament. It is something of a habit with me, developed, per- haps, in my early years at Gethsemani as I worked at becoming God-conscious. At any rate I was quietly saying *"El — Elohim — El Shaddai — Adon — Adonai — Yahwe — Yahwe Tsebha'oth — Elohim Tsebha'oth,"* when Alexie very politely asked me what language I was using. "The language of the spire," I said softly. "All those words mean just one thing: *God.*"

"All? — They did not all sound the same."

"*El* means 'The Strong One,' Lex."

"In what language?"

"Good question," I said and chuckled. "Let's just say Semitic; for it is found in the Babylonian, Arabic, and Ugaritic languages. That's going back — far back. Just about twenty centuries before Christ. Yet here we are using the same word and loving it for Him of whom it tells. Elohim is the plural of that word. And it is most interesting to note that the Jews, whenever they used this word about the one true God, would always have the verbs and modifiers in the singular. The Chosen People were monotheists with a vengeance. Yet, one is led to suspect that maybe the plural form of *El* has something to do with the Trinity. Just a suspicion, Lex. More than likely hind sight and reading into the text."

I then told the boy my fondness for the title *El Shaddai*. It is found in the Book of Job, and was used by the Patriarchs. I like the sound of it. I like its meaning. I hear it in Greek every Holy Week as that *Agios ischyros* rings out. *El Shaddai* tells me not only that God is All-powerful, but also that He is the Only Ruler, the Pantocrator.

I explained *Yahwe* as the Name God used of Himself when Moses made bold to ask Him, then told how the four Hebrew consonants, which spell out this Name, formed the famed and revered tetragammaton.

That led me to tell him how the Jews so reverenced this Name for God that they would not even pronounce it, but substituted *Elohim or Adonai* for it. I told the boy that this last was the plural form of *Adon,* which means "Lord," the Name we most usually associate with the Christ. That made me wonder aloud if Christ Himself had used *Yahwe* when the angry, taunting Jews once asked Him: "Who are you?" I admitted that I liked to think that Jesus said to them precisely what God had said to Moses by the Burning Bush. The solemnity of Christ's words seem to indicate this to me: "I tell you in solemn truth, before there was an Abraham, I *AM*" —

"I love the Names that begin with that *El*," I said: *"El — El-*

ohim — *El Shaddai* — They tell of Power — of Omnipotence — of Strength that brings worlds into being and holds them there. They are significant Names to use in these days when Technology is giving man so much strength and power. But when you want an atmosphere of holiness about you, when you want reverence in the air you breathe, use that holiest of all holy Names of God: *Yahwe* — for that tells you of God's transcendence as no other Name does or can; for *Yahwe* says that God is the lone Absolute, Unchanging and Unchangeable BEING — He is *Being* in all its plenitude, perfection, and power. You can add a word to it if you want to enter Heaven. Say: *Yahwe Tsebha'oth* — that word shows you God surrounded by those choirs of angels John tells of in the Apocalypse. It means *God of Hosts*. I hear that or, maybe more precisely, I hear *Elohim Tsebha'oth* 'Lord, God of Hosts,' when we sing the *Sanctus* of our Mass."

I could see that Forrester had some questions but just then the bell, summoning me to the chanting of None, rang out. "I'll see you after this Office, Lex — and maybe we can get to that 'more excellent way' I promised to tell you about." With a laugh I repeated, "Maybe."

As I hurried away I heard the impish, "Don't blame me. You're the man who has been talking Yiddish."

"Hebrew!" I corrected and hurried through the door.

None — the Ninth Hour — is a short Office, taking no more than fifteen minutes all told, yet when I rejoined Forrester, who was still under the ginkgo, I found myself in an altogether different frame of mind from the one that had led me on to course down the Names of God as found in the Old Testament. "I hear the call of the wild, Lexie. Lift that huge carcass of yours off that bench and let's head for the woods. Out we'll go by 'the postern gate' and see what we can see."

"Somebody's feeling frisky."

"Right! And you'd better get feeling the same way; for I'm going places this afternoon."

It was another golden day in mid-April. As we passed through the "postern gate" I found myself thinking of Robert Frost, for the sky was such a solid blue. It set me asking Alexie, the wall before me, and the entire world: "Why make so much of fragmentary blue?" I saw Forrester did not recognize the quote, so I went on with "In here or there a bird or butterfly?" He still did not show any sign of recognition, so I changed the words of the next line and said: "Or flower or blue-flame in Alexie's eye — When Heaven presents in sheets of solid hue?" My arms went up and out in a wide gesture. "Look at that sky!" I exclaimed, "and be washed afresh with beauty."

"Was that somebody's poem you were just quoting?"

"What a question from a major in Literature."

"I'm not going to major in English Lit, Father . . . I'm thinking of majoring in Philosophy. . . ."

"Don't! Don't you dare — unless it be Scholastic Philosophy."

He laughed at that and repeated his question about the quote. I told him it was from Robert Frost's *Fragmentary Blue*. That led us on to a brief discussion about Frost. I chuckled as we had to pick our way through a muddy stretch, made so by an overflow from one of our reservoirs. "If Frost saw us now, he'd most likely quote from his *Two Tramps in Mud Time:* 'You know how it is with an April day: When the sun is out and the wind is still, You're one month on in the middle of May.' "

"This certainly is a magnificent day! Look at those woods . . ."

I was happy to hear that exclamation, for my eyes had been on those woods since before we left that "postern gate." Spring had made them soft, shy, and alluring. The trees on the slope of the knob before us looked timid as they peeked out at us from fresh fringes of tender new green; the alfalfa field at the knob's base was lovely emerald bright with the sun. But just then a cloud came in front of the sun and a wind swept down from the knob's summit. I chuckled again, for Frost was still in my mind, and this sudden shadow and chill set me quoting more from his *Two Tramps in Mud Time.* " 'But if you so much as dare to speak' " I quoted and flashed a mock-serious look at my friend, " 'A cloud comes over the sunlit arch, a wind comes off a frozen peak, And you're two months back in the middle of March.' "

"Say! That's good!"

"Better than good, Lexie; that's excellent. That's Robert Frost!"

"You like poetry, don't you?"

"I love all that is beautiful. But let me tell you it is joy to share it with you, Lexie. When I had the boy from Northwestern here not so long ago, we took this same walk. I tried some poetry on him. You'd think I was using a foreign language. Intelligent youngster. But no such communications between us as between you and me. He did not know the classics as all who take the Liberal Arts course know them. That's a shame; for it takes much joy out of life. If I spoke to this boy about 'Helen of Troy,' he'd think I was talking about some girl from upper New York. To him 'Juvenal' connotes only one thing: a delinquent under twenty-one. Were I to mention 'Quintillian' he'd think I was talking about our national debt or the size of our foreign aid. To him 'Ulysses' would suggest only James Joyce; 'Oedipus' would make him think of a complex; and were I to speak of 'pius Aeneas' he'd think I was talking about some zealous monk. Now there's the difficulty with Education today — it allows for no communication between those who have been liberally — and of course I claim, truly —educated, and those who have been subjected to science, science and more science."

"You're wound up this afternoon!"

"Just the opposite — I'm unwinding." With that I quickly ran through the four years of study in a Catholic College of Liberal Arts and showed my friend the unity in the entire curriculum as I took as my thesis that Alma Mater took us "On the Road to Paradise." I saw Forrester did not recognize that as title to a song popular in the long ago, so I changed my phrase to "The Way to Happiness."

I laid the foundation for my thesis by asserting that an A.B. or an M.A. from such a College or University was a degree that not only truly designated, but designated truth; for anyone who has given himself to the courses offered in such institutions for four or five years will have come forth a master in the one art every human being longs to master: the art of living, which is really the art of loving. I stated the obvious when I told Alexie that no human being could be happy, could even claim he was alive, unless he could say that he was in love. God made us that way. Then I promised the boy that his soul would be deepened and steadily deepened as he went from the Poetry, so thoroughly taught in his Freshman year, to the "Queen of the Arts," Rhetoric, in his Sophomore year, then on to the Epistemology, Ontology, Cosmology and Psychology of his Junior year, only to have all climaxed in his Senior year as he reveled in the revelation of man and God in Ethics and Natural Theology.

The unity in the course approximates unicity since every subject taught converges ultimately into the mastery of the art of loving God — self — and fellowman — aright. Alexie manifested keen interest when I insisted that his Alma Mater would be giving him Literature not so much for language as for life; not only to teach him how to turn a phrase, set a sentence, and build a paragraph, but in doing all these to build his own character and shape his very soul. I promised him that through his study of Poetry he would get insight into depths within him that Depth Psychologists never see; for he would be set looking for the nobility in his being, the good, the true, and the beautiful. The Psychologists do not seem to know such things exist. This is the year when he would be made intimately acquainted with the art of arousing noble emotions, with thoughts as large as life, with the men and women who excelled in phrasing such thoughts in language that sang. "Never forget Augustine's keen observation," I said. *Cantare amantis est*— Song comes only from lovers." Poetry attunes the ear to the delightful rise and fall of rhythm, to the magic and melody in word sounds, to the rapture that can be wrought by carefully positioned cadences. But more, much more is taught in this year of Poetry than the marvel of music in words and phrases.

"The whole man is always being educated in the classical course, Alexie," I said. Then I showed him that his mind as well as his imagination, his will as well as his fancy, his whole soul as well as his exterior and interior senses would be trained as he learned how to look for the thought, imagination, emotion, and expression in every bit of poetry put before him. He would be being taught how to judge, how to discern, how to evaluate, how to appreciate. He would be shown how to analyse every form from that of a trifling triolet to the majestic structure of an Epic. But above all, he would be analysing his own soul even as he took some piece of genuine poetry apart. Further, he would have beauty poured over him this first year of his Arts Course, and would walk, as one has said, "covered with star-dust and with the winds of another world in his hair."

I promised him that he would learn how to dream — and dream aright — of all that is beautiful. I found myself telling Alexie that he could do what Francis Thompson claimed Percy Bysshe Shelley had done. He could "make the universe his box of toys, dabble his fingers in the day-fall, become gold-dusty from tumbling amongst the stars." I went on to say he could "chase the rolling world, run between the feet of the horses of the sun, tease the growling and kenneled thunder and laugh at its shaking of its fiery chain." I was unwinding all right. I told Forrester he could "make mischief with the moon, stand on the lap of Mother Nature, twine her tresses after a hundred different fashions until he found the one in which she looked the most beautiful." When I caught a twinkle in his blue eyes that was both appreciative and impish I quickly concluded, "But all this dreaming you will be taught is practical dreaming, the kind that sends you soaring from the visible to the Invisible, from the beauty in the creature to the bliss-producing Beauty in God. Above the beat of all poetry's magical music you are to hear the 'deliberate speed' and the 'majestic instancy' of the pursuit of your Lover, whom Thompson called The Hound of Heaven — God."

The deeper depths of his being that would be made manifest to him in his Sophomore year would be those of his mind, his emotions, and his passions. For Rhetoric is "Logic on fire." Here he would meet some marvelous ancients — Cicero, Demosthenes, Aeschylus, Sophocles — and would discover them to be quite modern; for man has not greatly changed since Cain and Abel were born. The same passions these ancients played upon as they exercised the "art of persuading," are the identical passions we must play upon today if we would move people. I used Cicero's well-known directive: "If you wish others to weep, you yourself must cry first." I indulged myself to the extent of saying, "It's a long ways from Madison Avenue back to the Appian Way, Lexie, but the rhetorical masters of the past utilized everything being used by the advertising men of the present. There is a striking solidarity as well as a striking singularity to man and mankind. Were that not true, literature would not live; for there would be no such thing as a universal appeal. We *are* all the same under the skin. God made us that way. That is why we can love and be loved. I speak of love here for in your Sophomore year you learn your own heart and the heart of mankind. As you become more keenly aware of yourself as you climax your study of the Humanities in this year, you will become ever more and more aware that every man is but your other self. That he breathes as you do because both of you have been breathed upon by God. What moves you can move him. What delights you can delight him. What anguishes your soul will anguish his. Thus you learn to love others and rightly love yourself and your God. There is a unity to the course. And, as you can see, it has to do with a trinity: God, yourself, and your other selves — your fellowmen."

I dwelt for a few moments on Drama as taught in the Sophomore year to point out, once again, the ultimate in all such study: sympathy, compassion, pity, fear, love for our fellow humans. "What was Hecuba to us or we to Hecuba that we should weep for her?" I asked. "Why do we soliloquize with a Hamlet and rage with a Lear? Why do we know pity and fear for each protagonist? — There is only one answer: our common source — the breath of God. He it is who shaped every human heart and set it beating in such a way that there can be such a thing as true Art — namely that based on a universal appeal. But now I go one step further, Lex, and say the Humanities teach you Divinity, and the solidarity of the human race shows you your oneness with God. Your pity for an Oedipus springs from the same source whence should rise your pity for God and His Christ. The Humanities as taught in Catholic Colleges fills the individual with a warm-hearted love for all mankind, for he sees each struggling human as a suffering member (actual or potential) in the Mystical Body of that Christ who 'will be in agony until the end of time.' "

When I came to speak of the Philosophy he would learn in his last two years I was tempted to tease him both about Nietzsche and the fallacy of thinking a History of Philosophy could ever take the place of a real *"cursus"* in Philosophy. But I grew conscious of the flight of time and of my desire to show him "the more excellent way." So I simply informed him that he would have his intellect honed in these two years to such a sharpness that with it he would be able to split hairs. But then I hurriedly added that it was not only his intellect that would be trained, but his heart would be purified, and his will properly oriented during his *course* in Scholastic Philosophy; for he would learn that this is a very practical Science — one that is to lead man not to this truth or that, not even to a set of truths, but to Him who is Truth. Further, it was such a *course* that he would be set studying the macrocosm in his Cosmology, and the microcosm in his Psychology. Both would lead him to the One who brought each into existence and keeps them there.

"You'll be studying yourself these years, Lex — and learning that the logic of life is the logic of love. You will be thrilled to find out, and be able to prove, that you are ever so much more than a mass of ganglia, a bundle of atoms, flesh, blood, and bone. Psychology will show you to be the responsible possessor of a soul that is simple, spiritual, and immortal, with a mind that can take in truth — all truth whether individual, universal, or transcendental; whether physical, metaphysical, or moral; and always able to recognize truth, thanks to an objective norm. It will show you with a soul that has a will that is as free as God is free — thus making you fully responsible as a person. It is a thrilling subject for it shows you your dignity — and, at least by implication, your destiny. You are a son of God with a home in Eternity."

The next two steps were made rapidly. Ethics, I said, would tell him his rights and his duties; but more, it would translate the gnawing hunger of his being as a longing for love which would be satisfied — when he would lay hands on God and have permanent possession of Absolute Good. Bliss is the goal of life. There is only one way to it — "Duty done spells sanctity, Lex. Sanctity spells eternal bliss. The way to Happiness is the way to God — and that way is labelled 'LAW.' . . . The Voice of Conscience gives us the Natural Law, and the Natural Law is but the Divine Law promulgated to us by that Voice. See what Ethics teaches? — LOVE. It will be followed by your course in Natural Theology which will teach you all about your Beloved whom we call God. Then you'll have your answer — at least in part — to that question you were mulling over this morning: 'What do we know about God?' You'll learn plenty, I promise. What is more you'll see how your entire course has been one, how all your truth is one, all your good, all your beauty are one; for you'll find God to be All.

"Your A.B. from Notre Dame, Lex, should qualify you as an Adventurer after God. That is the quest the liberal arts course in a Catholic College will set you on. That is why I say it does not prepare you for making a living, but rather for making a life. For life really has no other meaning: we must find God or fail to have lived. Having found Him we will have found Love. Now you can appreciate what a Jesuit called 'the most beautiful lines in the whole of the Old Testament': 'For what have I in Heaven? And besides Thee, what do I desire upon earth? For Thee my heart and flesh have fainted away. Thou art the God of my heart, and the God that is my portion forever.' Isn't that magnificent? And that's life. Nothing else is."

Forrester had been exceptionally silent during my exposition. Now all he ventured was, "I hope I get out of my course what you say can be gotten out of it. You've certainly made me anxious to have a real *cursus,* as you called it, in Philosophy. I hope I can unite everything."

"What I just outlined for you is the course in any Jebbie College. I believe it will be substantially the same at Notre Dame. I can hardly conceive of its being much different in any Catholic College; for this course is carefully aligned to the nature of man. And you can see, from what I have said about the ultimate aim of this course, how closely aligned to God man is. *Quis ut Deus* does have an answer, after all. It is: *Homo* — 'Man is like unto God' — God made him that way. I'm back to my spire again — and I can now show you 'the more excellent way. . . .' "

"I had forgotten all about it, Father. You did promise, just before you went to None. Is there a 'more excellent way'?"

"Indeed there is, and I'm going to teach it to you from that spire." We were on the same knob we had climbed Easter Monday. I pulled back a low-hanging branch and facing the Monastery said: "Look! . . ." The spire was shining brilliantly in the early afternoon sun. A tower of silver, topped by a gleaming cross, with no background save the wide-arched dome of a heaven that was gold-washed blue. *"El Shaddai,"* said I, "God the Beautiful! God the Good! God the Powerful! That spire is a veritable *Shekina* for this precious portion of God's universe. . . ."

"What's a *Shekina?*"

"The cloud by day, the pillar of fire by night. . . . The visible sign of the Presence of our Invisible God. . . ." I was stirred by the sight. "Believe me, Lexie, there are times — and this is one of them — when the sight of that spire reminds me so vibrantly of what Moses saw when tending the flocks of his father-in-law in the pasture land near Mount Horeb, that I actually expect to see flames envelop that spire, and hear what Moses heard from the Burning Bush. Isn't it beautiful!" In a slightly less ecstatic tone I went on: "I know I must sound like a dreamer, but I must confess there are many times a day, especially at sunrise and sunset, when I find that spire washed in sungold, that my every horizon seems to resound with the one word: God! But now for 'the more excellent way . . .' Look at that spire, but concentrate on the Cross. . . ." Alexie squinted as he glanced south to the bright radiance that gleamed from the metal which sheathed the spire. "Keep on staring at that Cross, as Chesterton might say, until you really see it. It will tell you much about our God — even about His inmost nature, and the social life He leads and has led from all Eternity; but it will tell you even more about yourself and your fellowman; about your worth . . ."

"My worth?" . . .

"Your worth — your work — and that of every man on earth — of every monk in that Monastery." I took a seat on the ground and pointed to the stump he had placed for himself Easter Monday. "Sit down and I'll educate you." Once he had lit his cigarette I began with, "Leon Bloy exploded once, as only Leon Bloy could explode, because a priest had written, in what he took to be humility, telling Leon that he, the priest, did not have the soul of a saint. — Someone said something similar in my presence recently. Know who he was, Mr. Forrester?" Alexie grinned. "Well, Bloy answered that letter with an explosion that told the priest that his admission had not only disappointed Bloy, but actually shocked him. For, the fiery Leon said, he was sure that his grocer, his scoundrel of a landlord, and the not-too-intelligent gendarme on the corner of his street, each had the soul of a saint. So have you, my young Stinker," I said. "So have I. Bloy was right. There is not a human being on earth this moment who has not the soul of a saint — not a one. Nor has there ever been one. Nero, Caligula, Napoleon, had the souls of saints. Marx, Lenin, Stalin, had souls of saints. Today, your Ian Smith, Kenyetta, Moise Tschombe, our L.B.J., Hubert Humphrey, and Dean Rusk — each has the soul of a saint. How those of the past made out, I don't know; but I have my doubts. How those of the present will make out, I don't know. But this I do know: you and I, Lexie, had better make out . . . or else. . . ."

Then I pointed to the Cross and said: "That Cross tells us how. . . . But have you ever realized that it tells you just what you are worth? The cross-beam reminds one of the beam on a balance, does it not?" Forrester nodded. "Believe me it is a balance — an exact balance — the only one God uses to weigh worth. It weighs you; it weighs me; it weighs the worth of every human being — and it tells us we are of infinite worth."

"Infinite?"

"That's what I said. That's what I meant. For that's what God said. I am sure it sounds strange to say that the tramp along the railroad tracks, the gypsy along the roadside, the man in the murderer's cell — each is of infinite worth. But it is not I who says it.

It is that Cross down yonder."

Forrester was silent.

"The Man who died on that Cross was Infinite, Alexie. He died there for you, for me, for each mortal who ever was, is, or will be. What can we conclude? What must we conclude? The price paid was infinite. The purchase made was the souls of humans. God made the purchase. God paid the price. God is Wisdom. What can we say but that humans are of infinite worth?"

"Hmmm. Is that clear, close reasoning, Father; or is it . . . well, what can I call it? Something sounds wrong. I thought only God was infinite. You and I, and every mortal man . . . we're just that: mortal — finite — not infinite."

"Good for you, Alexie. But now keep on staring at that Cross. Stare until you see its meaning. Leon Bloy was very fond of repeating the line of Scripture which says: *'Empti estis pretio magno'* — 'You have been bought at a great price.' He would immediately follow that up with: 'I should say so! You have been bought at the price of the Son of God!' — Now don't tell me that was human blood, Alexie. I know it was. But by this time I hope you know *actiones et passiones* — belong to the person. The Person who suffered the Passion which ended in Death on that Cross was the Second Person of the Blessed Trinity. He was Infinite. Need I say more?" When nothing but a narrowing of his eyes was my answer, I went on. "It adds up. We are of infinite worth; for an infallible God put a price tag on us. We were purchased by the Infinitely Precious Blood of His Only Son. Never sell yourself short. Never price yourself below the price God paid for you."

"But I still don't see. . . . No, I do not see . . . how you and I, finite creatures of clay, can ever be of infinite worth. . . . To me it doesn't yet add up."

"Maybe it will help if I tell you what a retreat master once told us: 'God the Father sees each of us humans through the red mists of His Only Son's Blood.' That Son was Infinite. We are His members."

"I know . . . I know. . . . But, still. . . ."

"O.K. — I'm delighted to find you refusing to swallow anything and everything that is offered you. Maybe that Cross will teach you today lessons not taught even at Notre Dame. Now let us think this one through: I've given you the Names of God as found in the Old Testament: *El — El Shaddai — Elohim — Adonai — Yahwe —* They revealed. That last one reveals His very Nature. But how distant they show our God to be from us little humans. The Man who died on that Cross revealed something new, something different about our God. He gave us a new Name for Him. He told us to name Him 'Our *Father.*' That was not bringing God down to our level, Alexie; that was elevating us far above the human. John the Beloved insists that we are not only *called* sons, but have been *really made such.* 'Like Father, like son.' God is Infinite. . . ."

"Of course, Father. I know He is Infinite. But I also know you and I are finite. Further, I know we have been made sons, but we have only been made *adopted* sons."

"Now we are down to the marrow, young man. Believe me that Cross is teaching you truth this afternoon. You haven't studied the tract on Grace in your Theology as yet. But I believe you know enough about this stupendous gift from God to know that it *elevates* us. That word is exact. We are *lifted up.* . . . Above the human. We are given a share in the very Nature of God, as St. Peter put it in his Epistle, *consortes naturae divinae.* The latest translation of that which I have read is 'sharers in God's essential nature.' Grace was won for us on that Cross. What Christ was by nature, we humans have been made by Grace. Believe me we are tremendous beings. We are heirs of Heaven; co-heirs with Christ. . . . Get that word, that reality, Lexie: *co-heirs!* We don't appreciate ourselves — and I'm using that word 'appreciate' in its proper meaning: putting a price upon. The Cross down there tells us the price — it is *Infinite.*"

My guest's face was sober, his head was moving from side to side. All I could think to do was repeat Bloy's favorite phrase: *"Empti estis pretio magno —* You have been bought at a great price." I repeated it twice, then asked: "Do you think God a poor bargainer? Was Infinite Wisdom unwary when He bought us back?"

"Bought us back from whom?" snapped Forrester.

I laughed at that, for I saw I had worked myself into a corner out of which it would not be easy to maneuver. "That's an excellent question," I said still smiling. "It has split Theological Schools for centuries — and still has them split. Some say from the devil. . . ."

"When did he ever own us?"

"That's also a good question. But it is much more easily answered than your other one. Let us begin with an agreement. We will agree that *re-demptio,* from which we get our word redemption, does mean 'to buy back.' Yes?" The boy nodded almost impatiently. "Next the question arises: From whom were we bought back? From whom could we have been bought back save from someone who owned us? But who could have owned us before our Baptism?"

"Not the devil surely. He did not make us. . . ."

"Were you in sin before Baptism? Were you dead to God when you were born? Did you not have to be reborn? resurrected from the dead?"

"Stay with this one idea of the devil, please Father."

"That's what I'm doing, Lex. You were born in sin. The wages of sin are death. Satan introduced sin into the world. He conquered your First Parents. He is Prince of this world."

"But did he own us? Did we have to be 'bought back' from him? This is a repulsive idea to me. . . ."

"Young man, you're making me think of things I have not though of in over thirty years. You've got me now recalling the various theories spun out by Theologians on Christ's great Act of Love, that Act of Redemption which we now call the Mass. Origen, St. Basil, and if I remember aright, St. Jerome, stressed this idea of *re-demptio* — or buying back. They had Scriptural grounds for it. And youngsters today speak of 'Scriptural Theology' as if it were a brand new discovery. Can there be any other brand? — It was my favorite, St. Paul, who gave these ancients their grounds. He speaks often of our being 'ransomed.' That's the same as 'buying back,' you see."

"Uh-huh."

"Paul tells that God sent His Only Son to 'ransom' those sold under sin; those who were in slavery. He explicitly states that 'Christ was given as *ransom* for us.' You see how natural it is, then, to be taken with this idea of *re-demptio* — and even to attribute the purchase price as being paid to Satan. He is the tempter to sin; and he and sin are closely connected. Yet there is something about the explanation that does not seem to explain. It seems to give Lucifer too much prominence; seems to place him almost on a level with God. Yet we cannot discard the theory entirely. Redemption does mean to 'buy back.' Christ paid the price — and that price was Infinite."

"Again?"

"Yes, again, Lexie. But with a new wrinkle this time. I begin with sin now. We men sin. . . ."

He nodded.   .

"We are finite creatures. But there is an aspect to our sinning that makes sin infinite. Stay with me now. . . . You told me you live in Walsh Hall, I believe?"

"I do."

"Am I right in supposing you have a layman working there who cleans the corridors and so forth, something of a janitor?"

"Of course."

"I suppose, further, that you have a priest at the Hall to act as Prefect."

"We have."

"And I know you have a priest as President of the University."

"So what?"

"So there's an 'infinitude' about sin."

"Yeah?"

"Suppose you were to insult the layman who keeps your corridor clean. You'd be guilty of a real offense, would you not?"

"If I did it deliberately, I'd be a cad."

"Good. Now suppose you were caddish enough to insult not the layman, but the priest who prefects your corridor. Would the offense be greater?"

"Greater than insulting the layman? I suppose it would —"

"O.K. Now let us suppose the impossible. Suppose you insulted the President."

"Suppose I did?"

"Three insults by the one man to three different men. Suppose the insult was the same in each case, would you feel more caddish to have insulted the President than to have insulted the Prefect, and more for having insulted the Prefect than for insulting the layman?"

"Of course."

"Why so sure?"

"It's obvious."

"Is it?"

"Of course it is. Anyone knows it's a greater offense to insult the President than to insult the Prefect or the layman."

"Excellent. Then my point is proved. There is an infinitude to sin."

"How so?"

"In the fact you just called obvious; namely, that we measure the guilt of an offense by the dignity of the one offended. God is Infinite. Sin is an offense against God. Therefore, sin is infinite. Therefore, the Cross up there . . ."

"I see the first conclusion. But that second 'therefore. . . .' "

"Obvious, Alexie. Infinite offense demands infinite reparation. An infinite debt can only be discharged by making infinite repayment. We're back to *redemptio* again. . . ."

"Yes, but with an infinite difference," broke in Forrester. "I see some sense in paying *God* back — but that idea of Christ paying an infinite price to the devil. . . ."

"I'll have to call you 'Anselm' instead of Alexie. It was St. Anselm who moved away from the explanation given by Origen, St. Basil, and, I'm pretty sure, St. Jerome. Anselm didn't like the idea of paying the devil, either, Lex. But there is something in the idea. We were captives; we were in sin; we were estranged from God. Being in the power of sin, we were somehow in the power of Satan. But Anselm focused on the Offended One — God. He showed that infinite reparation had to be made because of the infinitude found in sin. But only an Infinite Person could pay that price. Only God could redeem us. Is it not wonderful? Is it not a mystery of love? If God demanded full satisfaction for sin, there was only one way it could be done: God had to become man."

I paused there — for my own sake as much as for Alexie's. This Mystery of Love always shakes me. After a short while I felt I could go on without betraying too much feeling. "That Cross on my spire takes a thinking man further back than Eden, Lex. It takes us into the Eternity wherein God decreed to create man; foresaw his sin; then decreed to re-create him 'in Christ Jesus.' It takes us back to Eden, of course; for it takes us back to Original Sin. It was in Eden that the promise of the Redeemer was first given. That promise was kept. Hence, that Cross on my spire takes the thinking man back to Bethlehem, to Nazareth, to the Cenacle, out to the Hill of Skulls, down to the empty tomb, then up to Heaven where the Man, Christ Jesus, sits enthroned. . . ."

"Whew! You're going too far and too fast for me, Father."

"St. Paul will help you catch up. He named Christ the 'second Adam.' In doing that he enabled us to telescope all time; to fuse, as it were, Creation and Re-creation; to see all men in the One Man — Christ; to recognize the unity of the human race; and realize we mortals are immortal, we creatures of time are eternal beings. . . ." When I saw the danger signal in Alexie's eyes, I slowed down and said, "I'm only saying the same thing over and over: we are of infinite worth 'in Christ Jesus' . . ." When I heard myself using that phrase a second time, I stopped. . . . After looking long at the spire and the Cross atop it, I turned to Forrester and said softly, "I want to thank you. You've got the spire speaking to me this afternoon. . . ."

"I have?"

"Yes, you just caused me to use a phrase that tells all. . . ."

"Did I catch that phrase?"

" 'In Christ Jesus' — That's it, Lex. That tells all. The purpose of Creation — the purpose of Re-creation — the purpose of our Sanctification, and ultimate Glorification. We were made to be divinized, deified 'in Christ Jesus.' That spire is enabling me to understand St. Paul more fully — and even to hear St. John the

Beloved more clearly. He said: 'God so loved the world. . . .' That's us, Lexie; we are in the world of men. 'God so loved the world as to give His Only-Begotten Son.' We must be of infinite worth to God! Else He would never have given His Son for us. Redemption is a fact. Satisfaction is a fact. Substitution is a fact. Those are the three theories spun out by learned theologians — many of them Saints — to explain the Incarnation of the Second Person of the Trinity, and all it entailed. Ransomed we have been. God's strict Justice has been fully satisfied. Christ was the second Adam and became Sacred Head of the human race — but of a human race that was to be *incorporated* in Him. Oh, what meaning there is in that short sentence: 'We are His members.' What love of God for us it tells! Alexie, the Mystical Body explains all I have been stumbling to explain. . . . Look at that Cross. Listen to that Spire. Together they both tell of Love!"

The boy frowned. I went on: " 'I have loved thee with an ever-lasting love,' " I quoted. " 'God is love,' Lexie. God the Father 'so loved the world,' as you've just heard, that 'He gave His Only-Begotten Son.' God the Son so loved the world that you, and I, and every man can say what Paul said of himself: 'He loved me, and gave Himself up for me.' That's love — real love — sacrificing love — laying down life that the beloved might live! And God the Holy Spirit is the Spirit of Love. Indeed, God *is* Love. Study that Cross, Lex, and you will hear the very Trinity in Eternity — you will hear Them talking about you — and how They will show Their love for you. Indeed that Spire says: 'Love! Love! Love!' "

I paused only a moment, then went on with, "Listen and you will hear what John the Beloved put in the Prologue to his Gospel and what used to be the Last Gospel of every Mass. Remember: 'In the beginning was the Word . . . the Word was God . . . All things were made through Him . . . In Him was life . . . He came unto His own . . and . . . to as many as received Him he gave the power of becoming sons of God. . . .' What truths that Prologue speaks. What Love — Infinite Love — Eternal Love — it tells! Love of God for you, Lexie; for me; for every man born of woman. 'And the Word was made Flesh. . . .' " I stopped there. We both stood in silence looking down through the trees to the silver spire washed in golden sunlight.

" 'The Word was made Flesh,' " I repeated softly. "How God loves us men! But never forget, Lexie, that God became Man because He first loved God. Oh, I know we say *'propter nos homines'* in our Creed. And it is absolutely true. But it is not the whole truth. The Word was made Flesh for God before He was made Flesh for man. That had to be the case. For, as we have already thrashed it out: the first and final cause of all God's actions has to be God. The first and final cause of Creation, as we saw, is God's Glory. The first and final cause of Re-creation has to be the same thing — God's Glory. The first and final cause of your sanctification and mine — and our consequent glorification — if we want to be exact, Lexie, is God's Glory. That Cross down there tells of man's Redemption, of course, and tells it with truth overpowering; but it tells first, as we just realized, of God's Glorification. You made me think things through this afternoon, when you argued so stubbornly against the idea of paying back the devil. I'm glad you did. Now we see that it was God that Christ paid back, and hence, we know that He died for God's Glory. You and I live for God's Glory, Lex, and thanks to Jesus Christ and His Cross, we can give God His Glory perfectly. We can glorify Him in His own measure, which is always 'pressed down, shaken together, running over.' We can give Him Infinite Glory 'in Christ Jesus' — through His Mass! Now see how powerful you are — and how you can love God, yourself, and your fellowman aright. It is all a matter of *being* 'in Christ Jesus.' Look with my eyes, Lexie, and you will see not only the spire, but the whole Monastery, and every monk in it aflame. Yes, it is a veritable Burning Bush. It is aflame with the Fire He came to cast upon earth. With that Fire — which is Christ — we are kindled. It is a Fire of life and a Fire of love — Divine Love. Understand?"

"Not fully, Father. I'd be a liar if I said I did. But it is thrilling to hear one speak of God this way. . . ."

"The spire is speaking, Lex — or better, it is Christ speaking from His Cross. He speaks very well of God — and of man. He is

worth listening to. He tells of the Transcendence of the Father —
His Father and our Father, His God and our God. He is telling us
how much God loves us. He is saying that love craves union; that
God wants to be one with us. Think of that! Christ prayed for that
oneness at His Last Supper. To make an answer to that prayer possible He went out to a Bloody-sweat in an olive grove, then to a
Bloody Death on a Cross. And all that we might live! We were
born of the Cross, Alexie. Love gave us life — His own Divine
Life! Whenever you think of the Physical Body that hung on the
Cross, think always of the Mystical Body that came from His open
side. Realize that you are a member in that Body — a fact that
not only gives you your right, but your obligation to call God your
'Father.' Since you have that right and obligation, you have lien on
Heaven. You are co-heir with Christ; for you have been made
God's son. No longer just a relation to and from God — as Creation made you — an *esse a Deo* and an *esse ad Deum;* but now
you are a real Blood-relative of God Almighty. By that Cross you
have been deified, divinized, as the early Fathers of the Church
loved to say. Look at that Cross, Alexie, and let it tell you that you
are *sacred*."

I let that word hang in the air for a moment or two, then added,
"Sacred we are 'in Christ Jesus.' In Him we live, and move, and
have our being. In Him, through Him, and with Him we can love
God — self — and fellowman aright; for we will be loving as the
Only Son of God loved!"

"You mean by laying down His life for us?"

"I mean by taking it up again — and sharing that life with us. I
mean not only by dying for us but for living for us and in us —
and having us live in Him. How that simplifies, unifies, clarifies life
and living!"

"By being His member?"

"Yes, by being His member. Remember how I stressed the fact
that we are to give God glory? Christ is our answer. . . . Life has
only one purpose. Christ, the Only Son, showed us how to live;
for He showed us how to love — and that is life's real purpose.
Indeed He is 'the Way, the Truth, and the Life' — but even more

practically, He is 'the Light.' He has so lighted our way that we never need take a single step in darkness. We need never be confused. . . ."

As I saw Forrester ready to interrupt I held up my hand to check him; for my memory had clicked on that last word and brought to mind the Antiphon for Lauds on Palm Sunday, and I saw how it would simplify, clarify, and unify my whole afternoon's effort. "Alexie," I began quite deliberately, "had you been here Palm Sunday, you would have heard us open, or practically open, the Great Week with the chant of *'Dominus Deus auxiliator meus, et ideo non sum confusus'* — Which means 'The Lord God . . .,' that is Jesus Christ . . . 'is my helper, and *therefore* . . .' (Oh, get that word!) — *'therefore,* I am not confused.' No, I am never confused. How could I be, when He lights my way? 'He is the true Light that enlightens every man. . . .' He is 'the Light of men . . . and the Light shines in the darkness. . . .' Still shines, Alexie, but too many in your dark world do not grasp it; do not see HIM. Hence, they do not love — they do not live! They *are* confused. I hate the word. But I have to face reality. Yet I insist there is no excuse, far less any real need, for such confusion. Life is simple. God made it so. Christ lived it that way. He showed us how to live; for He showed us how to love. By word and example He taught us that *love is a union of wills.* Ever hear that definition?"

The question came suddenly. The boy, obviously, was not expecting it. He slowly shook his head and said, "No, Father, I don't think I have. . . ."

"That's the definition the spire gives. That's the definition garnered from the Cross. That's the only true definition of love: it is a *union of wills.* Your world speaks much of love, Lexie; but it does not know what it is talking about. You'd think it was all a question of the body. Sex is its idea. Love can be expressed through the body. Christ taught us that by delivering His Body up. But primarily, principally, and in full perfection, love is of the spirit. And Christ taught us that in Gethsemani and on Golgotha — 'Not my will, but Thine be done.' — That's the phrase that lights the way. That's the phrase that simplifies, clarifies, unifies. That's

the phrase that tells you what life's all about; for it tells you perfectly just how to love. And you and I know the Will of God in
our regard, Lexie. . . ."

"Do we? Oh, Father, that has been one of my difficulties —"

"Stop there. You've found it today. Paul, under Divine Inspira-
tion, under the direction of the Holy Spirit, told us: 'This is
the will of God — your sanctification.' I've told you 'Duty done
spells sanctity.' The duties of your state in life, the duties of my
state in life, the duties of any individual's state in life, is the Will
of God. Let's do those duties and we will be saints. Simple, isn't it?
All you have to do is be a freshman at Notre Dame. That's God's
will for you at present. You know those duties — in the classroom
and out of it. It's God's Will that you cheer the Fighting Irish on
to victory over Army, Navy, and Southern Cal. God's Will
that you celebrate those victories by dining and dancing after them.
All that is God's Will for you just as much as studying for exams.
So you see how simple it is to be a saint. Just be yourself — your
real self, not your pseudo-self! Paul has given you a fine directive,
Lex, when he said: 'Whether you eat or drink, or do anything else,
do everything to give glory to God. . . .' "

"Gosh! Whoever thinks of that at a game or a dance or a party?"

"If *you* don't from now on, you'll not live right, for you'll not be
loving aright. Did I not tell you more than once that you were
born for only one thing: to give glory to God? Paul clearly says
that you can do that at a cocktail party as much as you can in
chapel, provided the cocktail party is really part of the duties of
your state in life — and you act like a human; that is, deliberately
— God-consciously."

"Well I've never thought of that before. I can give God glory
having a drink. . . ."

"Do you know how to define 'glory'?"

"Hmm — Glory . . . You ask the most embarrassing questions,
Father."

I chuckled. "Bad habit, Lex. I'll have to break it. But if you'll
take Scholastic Philosophy you'll learn how to think aright — and
that means exact definitions. They define glory as *'clara cog-*

nitio cum laude.' That means 'clear knowledge which prompts praise.' Now follow these steps and you'll learn how to live. First God gives Himself glory. Oh, yes. Perfect glory. For He has the clearest of clear knowledge about Himself. He knows His transcendent excellence — His utter perfection. He rejoices in that knowledge. He cannot help Himself. That's a clumsy way of telling you how God lives and loves in the Trinity. For God expresses His knowledge of Himself in the Word — the Second Person, His Only-Begotten Son. Knowing one another perfectly, They see one another as Goodness itself — and They love one another and express that love in a Sigh — the Holy Spirit — the Third Person — the Spirit of Love. That's the Trinity. That's its Life: perfect Knowledge and perfect Love. But St. Paul tells you all Calvary is the center of the universe. That moment the very 'splendour of the Father's glory' in our midst. He offered Himself to the Father in our name. Thus 'in Him, and through Him, and with Him' mankind gave perfect glory to God. You know when. You know where. You know why. That Cross down there tells you all. Calvary is the center of the universe. That moment He died was the midmost moment of all Time. Thanks be to Jesus Christ, that moment has been made Eternal — and it is ours. . . ."

"Easy, Father. A bit more slowly now . . . a moment of time made eternal you say — and that eternal moment made ours. . . ."

"The Mass, Lexie; the Mass. That's the answer to everything for everyone. That is the simplification of all life and living; for it is all love. That is the unification of all our days and years. That is the clarification of our existence. You and I were born to give God glory. We can do it only 'in Christ Jesus.' He is the One who gives us the 'clear knowledge' of God, and furnishes us with the 'perfect praise' which makes for perfect glory — in His Mass. . . ."

"Don't shake the hold I have on a few basic ideas now Father. . . ."

"Shake it? Manalive, I'm tightening your grip. When Christ, at His Last Supper, said 'Do this memory of Me' He not only ordained His first priests, but made it possible for every human being to share in His Priesthood; made it possible for every man born of woman to make Mass his life and his life Mass. I never tire of that theme and that tremendous, truly thunderous truth. I am a consecrating priest. You are an offering priest. Together 'in, through, and with' Christ Jesus, the Only Priest of the New Law, we offer God Infinite glory, perfect praise. The climax of the Mass comes when the Consecrated Host is held aloft over the Consecrated Wine and the words of all words are spoken: *'Per Ipsum, et cum Ipso, et in Ipso est Tibi Deo Patri Omnipotenti in unitate Spiritus Sancti, OMNIS HONOR ET GLORIA.'* We, who are His members, are IN Him at that moment, and WITH Him, and THROUGH Him we offer *all honor and glory* to the Triune God. That is the climax — or it should be! — for the life of every human. It was for Jesus Christ. That is really what He said on the Cross. For, again, I insist He came first and last to give glory to God — to give Him back that glory we had taken from Him by sin. And what can you, or I, or any man do on earth better than what the Only Son did? And, as I said already, thanks to Him, we *can* do it; do it not only once daily, but from hour to hour, from moment to moment 'in Christ Jesus . . .' "

"Moment to moment. . . ?"

"You live from moment to moment, don't you? Well you should love God, and all connected with Him, from moment to moment. You should be giving Him glory from moment to moment. . . . And you can 'in Christ Jesus'; for He is offering Himself, and being offered, from moment to moment in Heaven and on earth — for He is being re-presented to God in and through Mass every split-second of the day and night as this orb of earth circles His sun. It is the Mass that matters, Lex; and nothing else really does. So long as we live 'in Christ Jesus,' we are in His Mass; we are in the greatest Act of Love possible on earth — and we are giving the greatest possible glory to God. We are living life at the highest pitch possible this side of Eternal Glory. Liturgy is life. . . ."

"I never heard that before, that 'Liturgy is life.' "

"Maybe not in those words — but that's what the spire and its cross say — and they tell truth. Life is love — or it is not life. Love is sacrifice — or it is not love. Sacrifice requires Priest and

Victim. Christ was both. Christ still is. So must every Christian be. Since we are His members, how can we be anything else? But to be so consciously, calls for *self-awareness* 'in Christ Jesus.' 'Be yourself,' Lexie, really means 'Be Christ!' He showed how to love. . . . 'Greater love than this no man has . . .' than that he be what he was made by Baptism — Christ! Thus will he love God — himself — and all his fellowmen aright. Be yourself — and you'll *live!*"

I turned toward the spire for one last look. " 'Michael' " — I said softly, then turning from it to Forrester I asked, "Did anyone ever answer the challenge of the Irish Archangel as did Christ? *Quis ut Deus* found, and yet finds, complete answer in Christ's Sacrifice of Love which won life for all human kind — not only in Eternity, but in Time. We live to God — or we merely exist. We can live to God aright only 'in Christ Jesus.' That spire tells you how to live, for it tells you how to give God *'omnis honor et gloria* — all honor and glory.' "

With that we started down the slope of the knob.

EPILOGUE • SENDING...HIM OFF WITH AN IRISH BLESSING

A L E X I E left the next morning. As I stood by his second-hand Chevy, I thought back on my own college days with their jalopies and racoon coats. Youth does not change, I thought. Styles vary, but the dynamisms are the same. I was just about to give the boy a blessing for the road when he smiled his impish Irish smile and said, "I have one last question before I get this show of mine on the road. . . ."

"Speak Lord, thy servant heareth," I said.

"All night long, as I reviewed our afternoon on the knob, the question kept popping back into my mind: 'Why did this monk ever leave the Jesuits?' Your whole talk yesterday was a Jesuit talk. 'In Christ Jesus' was all I heard. In fact, Father, I can sum up almost all your talking in that one phrase. Now satisfy this Stinker's curiosity: Why did you leave the Jesuits?"

"I thought that was obvious, Lexie. I certainly expected a sharp Notre Dame man to see just why. You can tell the world why I left. I had but one reason: to live in the society of Jesus. . . ."

I would have given a lot to have a candid colored camera at that moment and a sensitive recording machine to catch the expression on the boy's face and then the merriment as his laugh rang out.

188

"You leave the Society of Jesus so that you can live in the society of Jesus. That's good. And I really believe I know what you mean. . . ."

"Now the Notre Dame Stinker is showing some intelligence. To be honest, Lex, the Jesuit life was too hard. I came here where living in the society of Jesus is easier. You see, I'm brave, but I'm no hero. Ignatius of Loyola founded an Institute for heroes only. The Trappist life is ever so much easier to live. But when you get back to South Bend you can tell your Holy Cross Fathers that they'll all be Jesuits in Eternity. So will you. So will everyone in Heaven. For we'll all live in the society of Jesus forever."

"Now how about a last word, Father, something to sum it all up."

"Manalive! Haven't I given you enough words?"

"Capsulize, as you call it. You see, Father, you opened up with the Irish Archangel — and I understand some Gaelic. I saw the spire was saying 'God.' Yesterday, though, you got off into Hebrew, Babylonian, Ugaritic, — all Semitic stuff — and I'm not so good at those oriental languages. . . ."

"Yesterday I talked about what shows you that 'there is neither Jew nor Greek, neither slave nor free, neither male nor female; but all are one. . . .' "

"O.K. That was 'in Christ Jesus.' That's the Mystical Body. But now how about just one last word?"

"Well, how about *Eternity?*"

"How about it?"

"Lexie, though you were born in time, live in time, and will die in time, you are not a creature of time. You are an immortal being. Your Eternity has already begun . . . It began the moment you were conceived. You will never put off life and living. You will change your manner of life and your way of living. But you will never cease to live. . . . Never! — Therefore, your Eternity has already begun. Abbé Quoist has some telling lines about there being no such thing as dead people or as death. There are only living people — people living on earth and people living beyond earth. He's right. The thing you call death is just a passover. An

Easter! You go from life on earth to life after earth. You go on living. Good thought for those who live in this Age of the Jet and supersonic speeds. But what I wanted to say was what St. Augustine said centuries on centuries ago: *'Quod aeternum non est, nihil est'* — 'What is not eternal, is nothing.' Put the stamp of Eternity on everything you do in Time, Lex. I showed you how yesterday —'Whether you eat or drink . . .' — remember?"

" 'Do all for the glory of God.' "

"Good! There was a young Jesuit who had a very similar motto. His was in the form of a question. Aloysius Gonzaga used to ask himself about everything: *'Quid hoc ad aeternitatem? —* What does this mean towards my Eternity?' Pretty smart boys, these ancients. Maybe we moderns can learn a thing or two from them. But the reason I mention these two is because a wise Frenchman once said 'One motto *lived* brings sanctity.' So if you take Augustine's or Gonzaga's makes little difference, you'll arrive. Or take the one word you asked for: *Eternity —*"

"O.K., Father, now how about a last blessing for the road?"

"I'll give you an Irish Blessing, Lex. Remember how it goes. . . ."

"You gave it yesterday, Father — Yes, with all your talk about Christ."

"You're thinking of the Breastplate, not the Blessing. . . ."

"I'm thinking of that 'Christ before me, Christ behind me, Christ within me, Christ without me, Christ above me, Christ beneath me . . .' I've heard it a million times and more . . ."

"That's Patrick's Breastplate. I'll give you the Irish Blessing in short form: 'May all roads rise to meet you. May the wind be ever at your back. May the sun shine warm upon your face, and the rains fall soft upon your lands. And May God hold you ever in the hollow of His Hands.' Those Hands are hallowing, Lex. They will make you whole and Holy. There's the difference between the Irish and the Hebrews of old. They used to say it is a fearful thing to fall into the hands of the living God. The Irish intimate — and I explicitly state — it is a fearful thing to fall *out* of the hands of the Living God. I fear some of your contemporaries have. There is quite a bit of neo-paganism in modern times. Worse still, there is practical atheism as well as militant Communistic atheism. I was reading St. Paul's Epistle to the Romans this morning. It read like tomorrow morning's newspaper. . . ."

"Tomorrow's, huh? Not today's."

"Today's also, and yesterday's. Paul lists those things that make headlines: Suicide, murder, rape, robbery, revenge, rebellion. . . . But he does something more. He points to the cause of all such conduct, and does it with an accuracy no Criminologist knows. Paul pinpoints the deepest, the most fundamental reason for all these crimes and these criminals. He does it as no Depth Psychologist knows how. . . ."

"You make Paul quite modern. . . ."

"He is that, Lex, simply because he has truth, and truth is eternal — always timely, always up to the minute. As I read on this morning I could not help thinking that Paul had given accurate pen-picture of today's Commies. . . ."

"Yeah?"

"Yeah — in the first chapter of the Epistle to the Romans I read today about 'whisperers-behind-doors, stabbers-in-the-back, God-haters,' men who have 'overflowed with insolent pride and boastfulness, who have minds teeming with diabolical inventions.' Does that sound like a Commie . . ."

"Sure does, but it doesn't sound much like St. Paul . . ."

"That's from a new translation. It is exact and quite enlightening because of its modern diction. As I read on this morning I could not help seeing with ever clearer vision the parallel between pagan Rome in Paul's day and the world as it is in our day, especially that part of it behind the 'Curtains.' Paul tells of men 'whose minds were steeped in envy, murder, quarrelsomeness, deceitfulness and spite.' J. Edgar Hoover put out a bulky volume on the Commies of today and entitled it *Masters of Deceit*. Paul and J. Edgar do not seem so far apart, do they? Paul went on to say that the men of pagan Rome 'scoffed at duties to parents, recognized no obligations of honor, had lost all natural affections, and had no use for mercy.' Not a pretty picture."

"I should say not!"

"Yet it looks to me like a very sharp picture of many men in our modern world. But what I wanted to bring out was Paul's pinpointing the reason for such men and their crimes. He is precise, Lex, when he says: 'They gave up God, and *therefore* God gave them up. . . .' As I said, it is a fearful thing to fall *out* of the hands of the living God. How wise the Irish to pray: 'God keep you ever in the hollow of His hands!' But do you know what really burns me up is to watch the Commies stealing all our stuff. They use the 'housetops' we were commanded to use. They 'deny themselves daily' as we were told to do. They look for and work toward 'a City that is to come.' They have a 'faith' which they live. They are zealous. They are real 'apostles.' And we. . . ?"

"You did say it was a religion the other day."

"Pseudo-religion it most certainly is. Douglas Hyde, really a gung-ho Commie for most of his life, is the one who gave me the idea about the housetops, for he stated in public not too long ago that though 'the communists have the worst creed in the world they shout it from the housetops, while those who have the best Creed' — meaning us, of course, 'speak with a muted voice, if at all.' That, I fear, is too true. I hope you and your generation will right that situation, young man."

"My generation?"

"Exactly. The future is yours. No one can say just what the future holds, but he is a stupid man who cannot say who holds the future. It is you — *Youth!* Get your ideas straight. Get your ideals. . . . That's what youth needs. That's what youth has always been noted for. Idealistic youth is a proper designation. You and your buddies need no new prophets, Lex, no new evangelists, no new Savior. You have the Truth. Live it. I'm back to 'in Christ Jesus' am I not? The Way, the Truth, the Life. But He has made demands, given challenges, flung down the gauntlet. He said, and yet says; 'Follow Me!' Youth loves such challenges. Youth has always been ready to snatch up the gauntlet. Youth has always been idealistic. Catholic Youth should surpass all. For you know what sacrifices are demanded and the goal to which they lead. If you want to do something, be someone, achieve what is worth while, all you have to do is BE yourself, which means BE CHRIST. Do that and you'll change the world as God wants it changed — and prevent the 'Prince of this World' from taking over. I'm back to *Michael*. . . . You brought me back by asking for an Irish Blessing. God hold you in the hollow of His all-hallowing hands, Lex! I hope you hear from your golden dome up there in South Bend all we have heard from my silent spire. . . ."

"I've certainly heard plenty, Father — and it has been more than a pleasure; it has been enrapturing joy. I'm more than grateful. I'll prove it by striving to be all you said I should be and can be 'in Christ Jesus' . . ."

"That's the secret, Lex . . . God-consciousness — Christ-consciousness, true Self-consciousness, and hear 'Michael — *Quis ut Deus*.' . . ."

"You seem to favor that more than any other word, don't you?"

"I suppose I do, Lex. I believe the reason is that I see the need of a real devil-consciousness in your modern world. Michael, since he battled Satan — and did so successfully — seems *the* word for the modern man, provided men get all the connotations."

"Give the devil his due, eh?"

"Yes, you give him his due, Lex. Give him *Hell!*"

"That was his due, wasn't it?"

"That's what God gave him — and God is never wrong."

"Well, thanks again, Father. Pray me back to South Bend." With that he flipped down the little leather gadget which serves as shade for the driver. "Sun visor," I think it's called.

"Hold it!" I cried as he turned the key to start his engine. "Your sunshade just reminded me of how to keep you from ever growing forgetful of the one lesson I have tried to teach — that of simplifying, clarifying, and unifying. You know Jim Maginnis. . . ."

"I sure do."

"Well, on the sun shade in his car he has printed in large purple letters the one word K I S S. . . ."

"What in the world for?"

"For his wife and kids! I asked Jim just what you asked me when first I saw that huge KISS. Jim chuckled and explained that in his work as Economic Engineer he had lost many a prospective bit of engineering because he presented his case with so many details that it sounded complicated. He actually confused his prospective clients. After he had lost some valuable ones, he re-examined his whole approach and realized the necessity of doing what I've told you to do. So he printed those four huge letters where he would see them just before going into a prospect and they would say to him what I've been saying to you."

"Kiss?"

"No. Those four letters do not spell one word, they signify four. . . . Jim says he looks at them and hears the message: *K-eep I-t S-imple, S-tupid!* What he says about his business, I say about the whole business of your life, Lexie. I cannot call you 'Stupid.' But you are, and you have been, a Stinker. So I say K I S S . . . Keep it simple, Stinker! Now off you go with my Irish Blessing: God keep you ever in the hollow of His hands, Stinker."

"God bless you, Father!"

"Keep it simple, Stinker, and you'll be what God made you to be — a *saint.*"

As he turned up the tree-lined lane, with a wave he called back to me the words *"Michael — Quis ut Deus!"* I went into the house grateful to God for a most enjoyable visit.